24 FOOTPATH
AROUNI
ST.ALBAN ͻ

C000019124

With notes on places of interest

BILL FROST

Bill Frost

PUBLISHED BY ST ALBANS AND DISTRICT FOOTPATHS SOCIETY
(Reg. Charity 1039715)

First Edition 1988
Second Edition 1990
Reprinted 1991
Third Edition 1993
Reprinted 1997
Fourth Edition 2000
Fifth Edition 2004

INTRODUCTION

The St Albans & District Footpaths Society was inaugurated in 1967. The Society's booklet "Footpath Walks around St Albans" was published in 1971. This was followed by leaflets in 1978 which were revised in 1982. The book "24 Footpath Walks around St Albans" published in 1988 is now in its fifth edition, the maps and text having been updated.

The walks are circular using definitive or permissive paths and are generally described in a clockwise direction. The counter clockwise alternative makes an interesting variation. The map item numbers are used in both the text and in the "Places of Interest" at the back of the book for easy reference. In the text, compass directions will be helpful if paths are not easily visible on the ground.

To support our aims and avoid further loss of access, I hope that residents and visitors to St Albans will continue to walk in St Albans District thereby finding pleasure and enjoyment in what remains to us of our ancient heritage - namely our old tracks and paths.

The Society will be grateful for readers' observations concerning obstructions, overgrowth or insufficient waymarking. The Countryside Access Officer at Hertfordshire County Council should also be informed.

The Society accepts no responsibility for changes or errors nor for any accident sustained by walkers whilst using this book.

We wish all readers much happy relaxed walking.

Bill Frost
2004

Reproduced from Ordnance Survey based mapping on behalf of The Controller of Her Majesty's Stationery Office © Crown Copyright 2004 100017856.

Extracts from the List of Buildings of Special Architectural or Historic Interest are reproduced with permission of Her Majesty's Stationery Office.

FOREWORD

COUNCILLOR GORDON MYLAND
THE MAYOR OF THE CITY AND DISTRICT OF ST ALBANS

I am delighted to be asked to write this foreword to the Fifth Edition of "24 Footpath Walks around St Albans."

I commend many of the walks known to me over the years and the work of the St Albans and District Footpaths Society in their vigilance in ensuring the footpaths are walkable.

Whether you walk alone or in the company of other members of the society I wish you a safe journey and a warm welcome in the hostelries - most of which I have danced at with St Albans Morris Men.

Mayor and President 2004/2005

PREFACE TO THE FIFTH EDITION

The last edition of this book issued in 2000 has proved to be as popular as the earlier editions. Total sales now exceed 15,000 which demonstrates the continuing demand for the guide.

Since the last revision there have been further changes to the landscape around St Albans and, whilst we welcome improvements to some paths including the replacement of stiles by gates, it has regrettably been necessary to replace three of the walks due to their proximity to increasingly busy roads or difficulty with access at certain times. The deletion of walks does however give the opportunity to introduce new routes as described in walks 3, 7 and 23. Several walks have been renumbered.

A group of members has checked and rechecked all the existing walks together with the three new ones and the text and maps have been updated.

We hope that all readers will gain pleasure walking the paths with the help of this book.

John Howes, Chairman
St Albans & District Footpaths Society
September 2004

3

ACKNOWLEDGEMENTS

Thanks are due to the many members of the Society who have been involved in the preparation of this new edition. Peter Lawrence walked all the paths noting changes and a team of members checked the alterations to the text and maps.

Bill Frost has guided all the earlier editions to publication since 1988. He has carried out the alterations to maps and drawn new ones, thus continuing his involvement.

Once more we have used the cover design by Mrs Mavis Wynn-Ruffhead.

The continuing high level of sales has been maintained by Ian Kerr who has ensured that an increasing number of retailers stock our two publications.

MAPS

Further supporting detail is obtainable from Ordnance Survey maps available from bookshops. The relevant maps are :
Landranger No.166 Luton, Hertford. Scale 1:50000
Explorer No.182, St Albans and Hatfield. Scale 1:25000
Definitive maps to scale 1:10000 are available for inspection at Public Libraries. Reference should be made to these whenever there is doubt about the route or status of any particular path.

GRID REFERENCES FOR CAR PARKS

Each of the 24 walks starts from a car park that is located by its Grid Reference. To locate the car park, read the first three numbers of the reference along the top or bottom of the map in an easterly direction, i.e. from L to R. So 153 means from line 15, go 3 small divisions towards line 16. The last three numbers are read upwards using the lines on the L or R edges of the map, in a northerly direction. The intersection of these two directions gives the map location of the car park.

So G.R. 153,074
Locates the church.
The bridge is on
G.R. 158,075

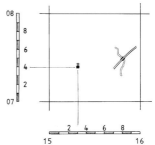

RIGHTS OF WAY ACT 1990

This act states that:

(a) Paths around the edge of a field must not be ploughed or disturbed
(b) Paths across a field may be ploughed and cropped but must be restored within 14 days
(c) Restoration means making good the surface to make it useable by walkers. Moreover, the line of the path must be apparent on the ground so that walkers can see where it goes through crops.
(d) The minimum path width must be 1 metre for a footpath across fields and 1.5 metres for a footpath around a field edge

If readers experience any problems concerning paths mentioned in this book, please notify the Footpaths Officer of Hertfordshire County Council and the Secretary of the Ramblers Association (see below). Quote the date, the Walks Booklet reference and the location given by a six figure Grid Reference or a copy of the O.S. map to highlight the problem.

Ramblers Association
2nd Floor, Camelford House, 87-90 Albert Embankment, London SE1 7TW
Tel 020 7339 8500 Fax 020 7339 8501

REMEMBER THE COUNTRY CODE

Be safe, plan ahead and follow any signs
Leave gates and property as you find them
Protect plants and animals and take your litter home
Keep dogs under close control
Consider other people

This is the most recent version of the Code issued in 2004. More information on the five points listed above is available on-line at
www.countrysideaccess.gov.uk/
Organisations can obtain multiple copies of the new Code by telephoning 0870 120 1273.

LEGEND

═══════	Motorway
═══════	Main Road
═══════	Secondary Road
= = = = =	Track or Lane
▬▬▬▬	Railway
— ▫ — ▫ —	Overhead Power Line (OHP)
— — — — —	Path
═══════ — —	Fenced Path
†	Church
×	Signpost
ʌ	Waymark. Yellow for footpaths, Blue for bridleway, Red for byways
⊢⊣	Stile
G	Gate
F. b.	Footbridge
PH	Public House
♀ ♀♀	Woodland Trees
L , R	The walkers left or right when walking the specified route
(N) (S) (E) (W)	Compass points
m	Metres
G. R.	Grid References
C .P.	Car Park

CONTENTS

		Page Number
Introduction		2
Foreword, Preface to Fifth Edition		3
Acknowledgements		4
Maps		4
Grid References		4
Rights of Way Act 1990		5
Country Code		5
Legend		6
Contents		7

		Miles	
Walk 1	Wheathampstead, Batford and Mackerye End	6.0	8 - 9
Walk 2	Wheathampstead, Gustard Wood and Lamer Park	4.7	10 - 11
Walk 3	Redbourn, Holtsmere End and Stags End	7.0	12 - 13
Walk 4	Redbourn and Flamstead	4.8	14 - 15
Walk 5	Rothamsted and Harpendenbury	3.5	16 - 17
Walk 6	Nomansland, Harpenden and Wheathampstead	6.0	18 - 19
Walk 7	Wheathampstead, Coleman Green and Water End	6.0	20 - 21
Walk 8	Redbourn and Redbournbury	4.4	22 - 23
Walk 9	Harpenden and Hammonds End	5.2	24 - 25
Walk 10	Nomansland, Symondshyde and Coleman Green	6.5	26 - 27
Walk 11	Redbourn to Hogg End Lane	5.5	28 - 29
Walk 12	Batchwood and Childwick Green	4.2	30 - 31
Walk 13	Sandridge and Ayres End	4.3	32 - 33
	Map of 24 Footpaths Walks Around St Albans		34 - 35
Walk 14	Marshalswick, Sandridge and Symondshyde	6.5	36 - 37
Walk 15	Oaklands, Smallford and Sleapshyde	7.3	38 - 39
Walk 16	London Colney, River Colne and Colney Heath	6.5	40 - 41
Walk 17	Colney Heath and Wilkins Green	4.5	42 - 43
Walk 18	Bedmond, Grand Union Canal and Nash Mills	6.3	44 - 45
Walk 19	Potters Crouch and Motorway Interchange	6.8	46 - 47
Walk 20	Park Street, Rivers Ver and Colne	5.0	48 - 49
Walk 21	London Colney, Old Parkbury and Shenleybury	6.5	50 - 51
Walk 22	London Colney, Ridge and Shenley	6.2	52 - 53
Walk 23	North Mymms and Redwell Wood	5.0	54 - 55
Walk 24	Colne Valley and Bricket Wood	5.0	56 - 57
Places of Interest			58 - 66
Bibliography			67

WALK 1

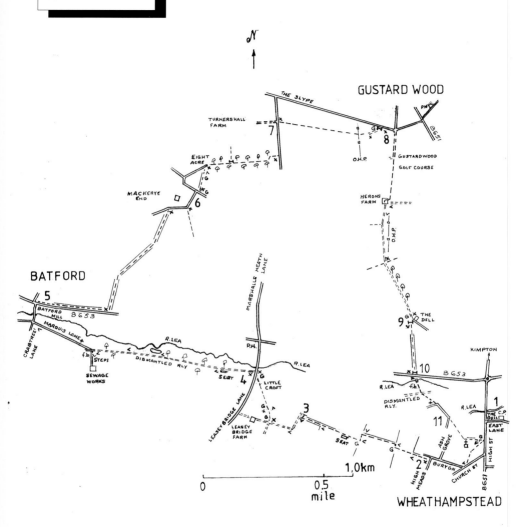

N

GUSTARD WOOD

THE SLYPE

TURNERSHALL FARM

7

8 GUSTARDWOOD
GOLF COURSE

O.H.P.

EIGHT ACRE

MACKERYE END

6

HERONS FARM

O.H.P.

BATFORD

5

BATFORD MILL
B653

MARQUIS LANE

CRABTREE LANE

f.b STEPS

SEWAGE WORKS

R.LEA

DISMANTLED RLY

SEAT

MARSHALLS HEATH LANE

P.H.

4

LITTLE CROFT

R.LEA

9 THE DELL

KIMPTON

10 B653

R.LEA f.b

DISMANTLED RLY.

R.LEA

1 THE BULL C.P.
EAST LANE

11

LEASEY BRIDGE LANE

LEASEY BRIDGE FARM

3

SEAT

ASH GROVE

BURY GN

2

HIGH MEADS CHURCH ST HIGH ST B651

WHEATHAMPSTEAD

1,0km

0 0.5
mile

© Crown copyright

Total distance 6 miles (9.7km)

8

WHEATHAMPSTEAD, BATFORD AND MACKERYE END

Park in public car park in East Lane behind the Bull Inn Wheathampstead, G.R. 178,141

1 From East Lane turn L up the High St (S). Go through the lych gate into the churchyard, cross to the (SW) gate. Turn R into Church St, and in a few metres R again along Bury Green. Note the old school building now offices. Go past Ash Grove and take the next turning L, High Meads. In a few metres take the path R marked by a signpost. This is part of the Upper Lea Valley Through Walk, notice the swan waymark.

2 The path (W) has a fence L and hedge R then crosses an open field. Go through the gate to a short R and L. Continue (W) with a tree lined hedge R. At the next transverse hedge turn L for a few metres to another gate. Go through and continue (W) along a grassy track over a field, then go between a wire fence L and hedge R.

3 At the next transverse track turn L at the swan waymark. This soon turns R and continues (W). This joins an access road leading to Leasey Bridge Farm. At the junction go through the kissing gate R along a path (NW) across a small field, to another gate with yellow waymark, go through this and continue (NW) to a third gate by a bungalow called Little Croft. This leads to Leasey Bridge Lane in which turn R to the bridge which offers views of the river Lea.

4 Return to the old railway track which is the continuation of the Lea Valley Walk and at the swan waymark continue (W) along the bridleway which gives further views of the river. The path continues to a bridge over the access road to a sewage works. Here turn L down steps and go under the bridge into Marquis Lane (NW). At the Marquis of Granby PH turn R along Crabtree Lane (N) and cross the river by the footbridge. Notice the thatched cottage at the junction with the Wheathampstead road B653.

5 Cross this road and turn R (E) on to the footpath on the far side. In 300m a signpost shows a path on L (N). Take this path uphill between hedges. It emerges on to a road along which turn R. The road bears L past Mackerye End House with its fine gardens and variety of trees.

6 At the next T-junction turn R and in a few metres is a footpath L (N). Go through two gates and a waymarked gap. This meets an access road (N) at Holly Bush cottage. Bear R to Eight Acre where a path goes R (E). This pleasant tree lined path emerges on to Marshalls Heath Lane along which turn L (N).

7 In about 300m opposite the entrance to Turners Hall Farm turn R (E) along a grassy track across a field. At the field corner continue ahead past allotments L into a gravel track which meets a road called the Slype. Here turn R for Gustard Wood Common (E). Note the house called "Hogs Island" L.

8 At the cross roads continue (S) along the access road to the cottages R, with golf course L. This continues (S) into a wide track leading to the access road to Herons Farm. Turn R into the farm, then L to a wide gravel track (S). This track continues (S) past a signpost to the iron gate at Dell Farm.

9 Do not go along the road, instead cross the stile just before the house called "The Dell" and continue (S) across the field to a stile on the B653 road.

10 Cross the road to an asphalt footpath that crosses the river Lea by a footbridge. This continues (SE). At the road junction turn L.

11 When this road turns R, the footpath continues (SE) across a playing field, into the churchyard. Either way round this Parish Church of St Helens leads to the lychgate. Turn L down High Street back to the car park.

WALK 2

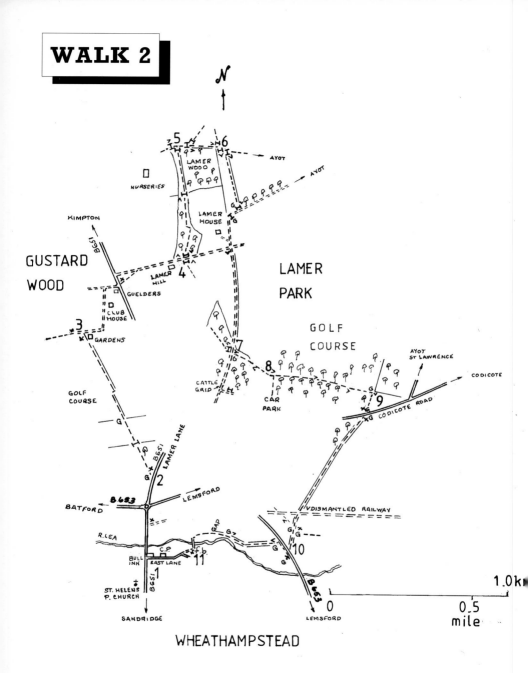

N

5
6
LAMER WOOD
AYOT
AYOT
NURSERIES
KIMPTON
LAMER HOUSE
GUSTARD
WOOD
LAMER MILL
4
LAMER PARK
GUELDERS
CLUB HOUSE
3
GARDENS
GOLF COURSE
7
GOLF COURSE
AYOT ST LAWRENCE
CODICOTE
8
CATTLE GRID
CAR PARK
9
CODICOTE ROAD
LAMER LANE
BG51
2
LEMSFORD
B653
BATFORD
DISMANTLED RAILWAY
R.LEA
10
BULL INN
C.P.
EAST LANE
11
1
ST. HELENS P. CHURCH
BG51
B653
SANDRIDGE
LEMSFORD
0

1.0 km

0.5
mile

WHEATHAMPSTEAD

© Crown copyright

Total distance 4.7 miles (7.6km)

WHEATHAMPSTEAD, GUSTARD WOOD AND LAMER PARK

Park in public car park in East Lane behind the Bull Inn, Wheathampstead. G.R. 178,141

1 From car park return (W) to High Street B651, cross the road and turn R along Mill Walk. Continue over roundabout into Lamer Lane B651 (N). In about 200m, opposite the large wrought iron gates R, turn L at a signpost and go through a kissing gate.

2 Take this path L and continue over a meadow (N). Cross the stile in the next crossing hedge, take the clear path ahead across a field (N) to a kissing gate. This leads to the golf course L, continue with fence and hedge R.

3 At the signposted transverse track, turn R (E), the track bears L (N) past the club house R. At the T-junction turn R, and at "Guelders" with its post box, cross Lamer Lane to the signpost opposite. Continue past weather boarded cottages into an asphalt road (NE) in Lamer Park.

4 Pass "Lamer Hill" and after a further 40m at the boundary of the wooded garden R, turn L (N) over a stile to a footpath through the woods. Cross a stile in a transverse fence, continue (N) following a wire fence R.

5 At the boundary of the woods cross a stile. Ignore the stile L, instead turn R (E) following the edge of the wood. Cross the stile (E) ignoring a stile L. Continue between wire fences, and turn R to cross another stile at the corner of the wood, again ignoring a stile L.

6 Continue (S) with wire fence L to an iron gate and stile in L corner of the meadow. Note the fine avenue of trees on L. Turn R along this avenue and in a few metres cross a stile on to an asphalt road where turn L (S). At the crossing of tracks on the corner of Lamer House, bear L along the wide gravel track (S) towards woodland with high wire fence L.

7 Immediately on entering the woodland, turn L (E) through the gate in the wire fence, along a footpath on the inside edge of the wood. Continue (E) along a line of pines past the golf car park R.

8 Ignore the path R, bear L and continue ahead through woodland (E) keeping close to an avenue of beeches R. Follow the waymarks as the path bears R, at the edge of the wood cross the golf course (E) up a slope.

9 At the junction of two areas of woodland turn R through the gate in the high wire fence. Keep close to the fence R and continue (S) to the signpost at the Codicote Road. Cross the road to a wide gravel track (S) past young trees and wire fence R. Continue across the dismantled railway, down to a gap by an iron gate. Go under the bridge carrying the Cory Wright Way.

10 In 60m after the bridge, turn R by the nearby signpost, to the fenced bridleway which follows the road (NW). Turn L through the gate at the swan waymark, and continue (W) between wire fences with views of the river L. At the gap in the hedge, is a permissive path leading to the river bank. A clear path follows the river to a footbridge.

11 Cross the bridge on to an asphalt track (W) passing an outbuilding. Continue along Meads Lane, past Mead Hall and so to the car park.

WALK 3

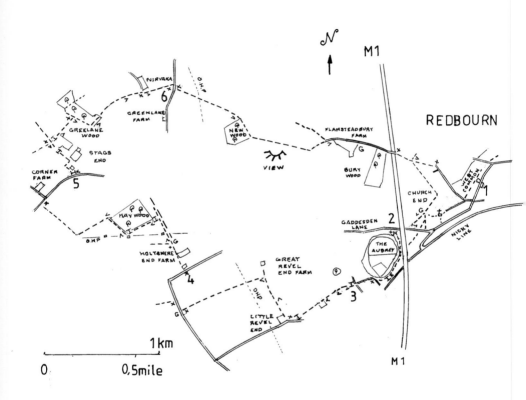

© Crown copyright

Total distance 7.0 miles (11.2km)

REDBOURN, HOLTSMERE END AND STAGS END

WALK

3

Park in car park on Redbourn Common near the cricket pavilion opposite the old school. G.R. 103,119

1 From the pavilion take the asphalt path (SW) across West Common into Church End, continue along to Redbourn Parish Church, take path across in front of church into cemetery. In the cemetery turn R (NW) at the first crossing path to reach a gate. Here turn L and go diagonally across a field towards far side of wooden fence near motorway and cross a stile into Gaddesden Lane. Turn R, go under bridge and immediately turn L.

2 Go over stile and follow a well defined path nearly parallel to the motorway (S) around The Aubreys fort, cross a stile and go directly across the hotel access road to a path between hedges (SW). Continue bearing R along a hedged path to meet a gravel crossing track. Turn R along this track until meeting a transverse track, turn R then immediately L (SW) on a path between houses to a stile.

3 Cross and bear R (W) across a field to a group of oak trees, turn L (SW) at waymark. Continue with hedge R, then fence L and hedge R. Pass farm L to an open field, cross and aim for pylon straight ahead. On reaching a stile L do not cross but turn R (NW) with hedge and fence L, through a crossing hedge and aim for copse R and farm buildings ahead. At waymark on farm track turn L (SW), continue under pylon cables to reach a gate at road junction. Turn R along road to a T-junction at the entrance to Holtsmere End.

4 Go up this private road past Holtsmere Farm R, continue up to a gated path junction, take a clear path L (NW) through the wood to a wooden crossing barrier, go through turn L and go over stile. Continue (SW) with Hay Wood R to another stile, go over turn R (NW) on to a bridleway with wood R. At end of wood turn L (SW), follow this track to a crossing hedge, turn R (NW) continue to Cupid Green Lane at a hedge gap. Turn R (NE) along lane, pass Gaddesden Row L. Continue along Gaddesden Lane to Stags End Cottage Barn R.

5 Take bridleway L (NW), this path zig zags around Stags End House to a stile, cross and go through a small copse to a signposted crossing path. Turn R (NE), cross stile continue with wood R, then downhill to Greenlane Wood. Turn R (SE) to the corner of wood, turn L (NE) uphill with wood L. Continue with hedge L to a waymark post, bear R across field to a hedge gap in Green Lane (track). Turn R and follow track past Nirvana farm to meet a crossing road at end of drive.

6 Turn R then in 50 m turn L (SE) along path with hedge L, under pylon cables towards wood R. Continue with wood R, at the corner of wood track veers L between fields to join a transverse bridleway. Turn R (E) past Flamsteadbury Farm, this leads to a bridge over the M1. Cross this into Flamsteadbury Lane and on to West Common and the car park.

WALK 4

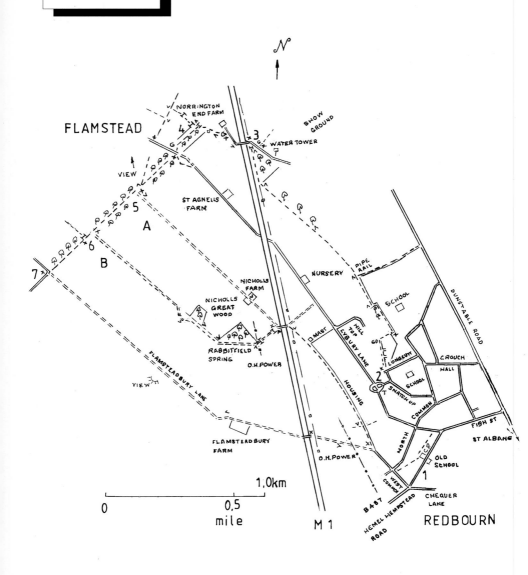

FLAMSTEAD

NORRINGTON END FARM

4

3 WATER TOWER

SHOW GROUND

VIEW

ST AGNELLS FARM

5

A

6

B

7

NURSERY

PIPE RAIL

SCHOOL

DUNSTABLE ROAD

NICHOLLS FARM

NICHOLLS GREAT WOOD

RABBITFIELD SPRING

O.H.POWER

HILL TOP

LYBURY LANE

MAST

GDI

HOUSING

2

SCHOOL

LONGBUTT

CROUCH HALL

SNATCH UP

COMMON

FLAMSTEADBURY LANE

VIEW

FLAMSTEADBURY FARM

O.H.POWER

NORTH COMMON

WEST COMMON

FISH ST

ST ALBANS

GP

OLD SCHOOL

1

1,0km

0   0,5
         mile

M 1

BAST

HEMEL HEMPSTEAD ROAD

CHEQUER LANE

REDBOURN

© Crown copyright

Total distance 4.75 miles (7.6km)
Alternative A 4.0 miles (6.4km)
Alternative B 4.6 miles (7.5km)

REDBOURN AND FLAMSTEAD

**Park in car park on Redbourn Common near the cricket
pavilion, opposite the old school. G.R. 103 119**

1 From the pavilion take the asphalt path (NE) to the next crossing road Lybury Lane, along which turn L. Continue (NW) passing Brache Close and Down Edge to a circle of houses. Turn R into The Terrace and Ridge Down, passing the telephone box, then L into Snatchup to its junction with Long Cutt. Cross to the path opposite by the signpost to Flamstead.

2 This path crosses a play area and goes into the Hilltop housing estate. At number 60 turn R on to a path (E) and in 100m turn L to follow the school's playing field fence R. This clear track goes across fields (NW) with a water tower ahead. Cross under the power lines and at the M1 boundary fence continue into a path between this fence and a plantation R. Continue (N) along the fence to a stile and signpost in a farm road.

3 Cross this stile and turn L along the road towards Norrington End Farm. Cross the bridge over the M1, and in about 150m, just before a cottage turn L and go through a kissing gate at a signpost. Cross a small field (SW) and at the cottage boundary turn R at waymark into a meadow (NW). Look for a local power line post with a wood behind it and continue down to a corner of this wood (NW).

4 Here cross a stile and follow a clear path (SW) inside the wood between wire fences. (This is a permissive path, if closed turn R over adjacent stile, go downhill and at the bottom turn L on to a bridleway to Lybury Lane. Here turn L and in 150m turn R up a track to rejoin walk at Item 5). This emerges into Lybury Lane at a gate. Cross the lane and enter a green track opposite (SW) which can be muddy in wet weather. At the junction with another track note the fine view of Flamstead (N) through a gap in the hedge.

5 In a few metres (SW) at a junction, ignore the wide track which goes (SE) to Nicholls Farm, but continue along the track (SW) for about 400m to a signpost L.

6 Still on this same track (SW) continue to a road corner with a sign for Flamsteadbury.

7 Here turn L (SE) along the access road which crosses open fields to Flamsteadbury Farm and leads to a bridge over the M 1. Cross this into Flamsteadbury Lane on to West Common and the car park.

Alternative A

At item 5 turn L along the wide track (SE) which goes through Nicholls Farm. Cross the M1 bridge, and at the power line take the path (SE) along the boundary fence of the housing into Flamsteadbury Lane, on to West Common and the car park.

Total distance 4 miles (6.4km).

Alternative B

At item 6 turn L at signpost (SE) along a hedge L past the boundary of Nicholls Great Wood L. Soon where the wood boundary goes sharp R, look for a clear winding path (SE) inside the edge of the wood. Emerge from the wood and at the far corner by a local power line, a stile leads to a path (NE) and over a second stile to a bridge over the M1. Cross this and at the power line take the path (SE) along the boundary fence of the housing into Flamsteadbury Lane, on to West Common and the car park.

Total distance 4.6 miles (7.5 km).

WALK 5

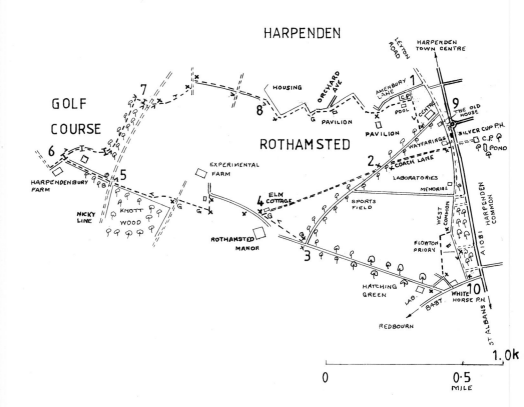

HARPENDEN

GOLF

COURSE

ROTHAMSTED

© Crown copyright

Total distance 3.5 miles (5.6km)
Alternative via Hatching Green
4.0 miles (6.4km)

ROTHAMSTED AND HARPENDENBURY

Park in public car park (parking fee) in Amenbury Lane, Harpenden.
G.R. 133,141 or on Harpenden Common G.R. 137,138.

1 (A) From the car park take the footpath (S) following signs for the sports centre into Rothamsted Park. Turn R along the fine avenue of trees (SW) to a crossing track marked by concrete posts, item 2

(B) If parked on the Common, cross the main St Albans road into Coach Lane alongside "Wayfarings". Continue along this lane to item 2.

(C)**Alternative Loop:-** from map item 9, the main entrance to Rothampsted Park, some interesting buildings are visible along Leyton Road (S) and West Common. At the junction with Redbourn Lane B487, map item 10, turn R, go past the White Horse PH and Hatching Green. Turn R into the access road leading to Rothampsted Manor to rejoin the walk at item 3.

2 In a few metres take the fork R at the bridleway signpost along a wide track leading to Elm Cottage, item 4. **Alternatively** you may prefer to continue along the avenue of trees (SW) to a road junction item 3.

3 At this junction turn R and in a few metres note a gate and sign R. Go through this gate, keep to the fence R, and continue to Elm Cottage at a signpost item 4.

4 A few metres (S) of the cottage is a transverse road, turn L along it if you wish to view Rothamsted Manor. Retrace your steps and continue along this road (NW) past the cottage R. In a further 500m the road turns sharp R, here turn L along a bridleway (S). In about 110m turn R at a signpost. Continue (W) through two gates, cross a farm road and go towards a wood (W). The path now bears R at the wood and keeps on along the edge of Knott Wood (NW) to the 'Nicky Line', a disused railway track.

5 Cross this and go down a path between fences (NW). Where this track turns sharp L note a stile on R.

6 Cross this stile, continue (NE) over pasture and another stile with fence L. At the edge of the wood is another stile L. Cross this and keep to a path (N) through this wood adjacent to the golf course. On emerging from the wood at a waymark sign, turn R towards the power line. Cross a stile and go along the edge of a field (E) and in a few metres reach the 'Nicky Line' again.

Alternatively a slightly shorter route is to go from item 5 along the Nicky Line direct to item 7.

7 Cross this and continue (E) along a wide well-marked track with fence and hedge R. This bends (NE) to a farm road in which turn L. In a few metres turn R (E) along a hedge R.

8 At the end of the fields turn R at a signpost along a boundary hedge L bordering housing. Go through a gap in the hedge, turn sharp L, follow on around the headland to a gate into the park. Keep alongside a hedge L, go past the cricket pavilion and the gate in Orchard Avenue. Continue with hedge L until reaching a second pavilion R. Take the gravel track past the tennis courts L, and the sports field R. Finally go past the swimming pool R and return to the car park L.

17

WALK 6

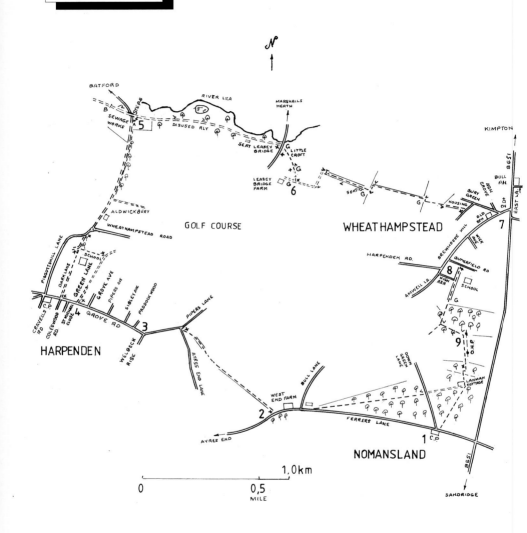

© Crown copyright

Total distance 6.0 miles (9.7km)

NOMANSLAND, HARPENDEN AND WHEATHAMPSTEAD

Park in public car park on Nomansland Common, at junction of Down Green Lane and Ferrers Lane. G.R. 171,124

1 Go up Down Green Lane (N) for about 200m to a transverse bridleway. Turn L at the waymark post (W) through woodland. Avoid forks and follow path straight ahead (W) into Ferrers Lane. Go past the junction with Bull Lane and West End Farm .

2 After 150m past the farm, turn R along a wide track at a signpost (NW). This continues with hedge L into a road junction with Pipers Lane.

3 Continue (W) along Pipers Lane on a footpath R, passing Welbeck Rise L. Then along Grove Road to the fifth turning R signposted Green Lane.

4 Turn R along Green Lane (N) passing a school L, continue uphill to a signposted path L. Turn L along path through trees between school L and allotments R, this joins Dark Lane. Turn R on to an asphalt path through trees and emerge on to Piggottshill Lane, here turn R to a small roundabout. Cross and continue past Aldwickbury golf course R where the path narrows and goes downhill. Further on there is a pleasant path through trees parallel to road.

5 At the sewage plant, note the old railway bridge ahead. Go up the steps R on to the old railway track, turn R (E). This is part of the Upper Lea Valley Walk, and the track continues (E) to Leasey Bridge Lane at the swan waymark. At the lane divert to L to view the river from the bridge. Then retrace your steps (S) up the lane passing the Gatehouse L. At the bungalow called 'Little Croft' turn L at the signpost. Go up the drive R through a swing gate and bear L across the field along a clear path (S). Go through another gate, then with hedge R a third gate into the farm access road. Note Leasey Bridge Farm R.

6 Turn L (E) along a wide track with a wire fence on each side. This track makes a short L and R round a field, then goes E at the waymarked post with hedge L. Go through a swing gate in the hedge, turn L and in a few metres R (E) following a hedge L. Continue through another gate to the boundary of the housing L and wooden fence R. The path meets a road at a signpost. Turn L and at the junction with Bury Green turn R, go downhill into Church Street.

7 Turn sharp R round the old school now converted to offices, go up Brewhouse Hill, take the second turning L which is Butterfield Road (E).

8 In about 200m note a signpost R at a path which goes S along the boundary of a former school L. This clear path continues into woodland, then turns L (E) at a waymark along the inside edge of the wood, to a power line post.

9 At this post turn R along the edge of a field following the power line. The path enters woodland past a signpost. Continue (S) through the woods following a path marked with white arrows to Lanman Cottage. Ignore the track R, continue (SW) through the woods back to Ferrers Lane at the car park.

10 **Note:**   Alternative car parking is available starting from East Lane car park in Wheathampstead near item 7, or from Cravells Road car park at junction with Grove Road in Harpenden near item 4.

WALK 7

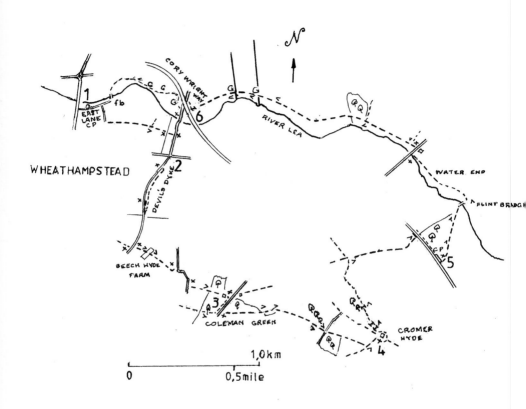

1,0 km

0   0,5 mile

© Crown copyright

Total distance 6.0 miles (9.7km)

WHEATHAMPSTEAD, COLEMAN GREEN AND WATEREND

Park in public car park in East Lane behind the Bull Inn, Wheathampstead, G.R. 178,141

1 Turn L (E) on leaving car park past Mead Hall L. Turn R up East Lane into the recreation ground. Head (E) across grass towards sports pavilion, continue along path with hedge R. Continue between fence L and hedge R to a tarmac road. Here turn R uphill to Marford Road, cross over and continue up Dyke Lane to the entrance to Devils Dyke L.

2 Enter and keep to the bottom of the Dyke. At the southern end of the Dyke, turn R up a bank. The path curves R at the top into Dyke Lane. Turn L along the lane to a signposted path into Beech Hyde. Turn L into the farm keeping to left hand track through farm, over a stile and continue to a road junction. Turn R then in a few metres L at Herts Way signpost. Continue uphill (SE) across field to a wood. Go through the wood and exit by a cottage L on to the green. Turn R at signpost then go ahead for 50m then L to cross Coleman Green Lane.

3 Go through barrier gate, turn L, take path (E) with woods L. Go through a gap, woods now on R. Turn R at the end of wood, then (E) diagonally uphill to the third group of holly bushes. Bear R keeping hedge L, cross a transverse path, continue (SE) with wood R to a gap. Go through with hedge L to a waymarked crossing path. Turn L through hedge (NE) across field to Cromer Hyde House.

4 Here go through a large gate into the gravel entrance, go past the house L to a stile just beyond a gate. Cross and continue to a double stile (NW) across the field. Bear R across field to second oak tree. Continue with fence L to a stile, cross and follow path, hedge L, downhill. Turn R at bottom and continue along Drovers Way Lane to Marford Road B653. Turn L up to the road. Cross with care, turn R using grass verge to the car lay-by in 150m.

5 Enter car park, footpath starts at centre over a stile into woods on a well defined path downhill (N) to Flint Bridge over the river Lea. Cross bridge then turn L along a path (NW) with fence L. This follows the river L and emerges on to a road at Waterend with ford L. Turn R, then in a few metres turn L (NW) opposite the large Elizabethan house. This gravel bridleway follows the river with hedge L. In 500 m at a bend, continue ahead (W) with wood R and then at end of wood, hedge L meadow R to a gate. Go through this gate into water meadows (W). Continue, bear L at fork to a gate, through gate to a signposted stile by the Cory Wright Way.

6 Turn R along a fenced path, down steps, go under the bridge. In 50 m turn sharp R (NW) at a gate into a fenced path to another gate. Continue (W) through a metal gate then bear L into a hedge gap to a permissive path following the river L. Cross the footbridge L and bear R along Meads Lane and East Lane to the carpark.

WALK 8

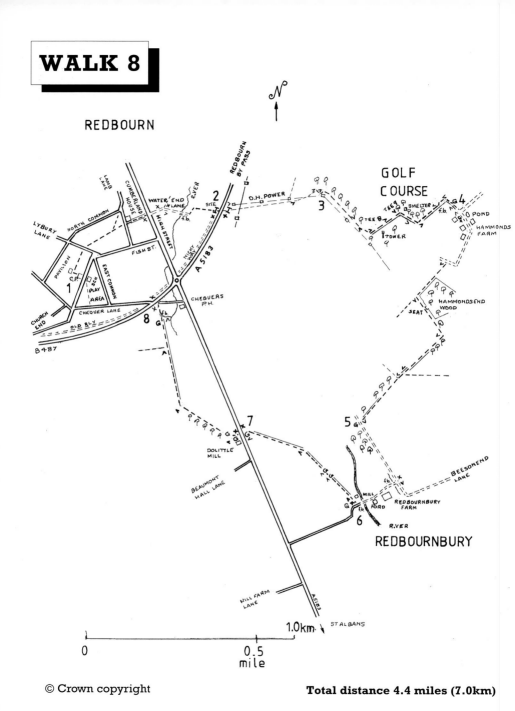

REDBOURN

REDBOURNBURY

GOLF COURSE

1.0km

0   0.5
              mile

© Crown copyright

Total distance 4.4 miles (7.0km)

REDBOURN AND
REDBOURNBURY

**Park in public car park on Redbourn Common, near cricket
pavilion opposite the old school. G.R. 103,119**

1 From the pavilion take the clear asphalt path (NE) across the common. Cross Lybury Lane and keep straight ahead to a transverse road. Continue past Cumberland House L along a path (E) between brick walls called The Ruins, to the High Street. Cross to Waterend Lane opposite. Go down this lane, cross the River Ver by the footbridge and in about 40m the path turns L then in a few metres R. Go past the path L, continue alongside a green metal fence to the old railway track called the Nicky Line. Cross this at the stile and continue to the by-pass.

2 Cross the by-pass to the steps opposite, go over the stile to a field path. Continue uphill (E) along the path parallel with the single pole power line to a hedge gap by a power pole, continue ahead with hedge R to waymark post at woods. Turn R.

3 At the point where the power line changes direction, turn L, go through the hedge at the corner pole, by a waymark sign. The path continues R (SE) through woods bordering the golf course, and emerges on to the edge of the course. Turn R to Tee 8 (Ramblers Risk.) then L (E) and continue close to hedge R. Approximately 25m past Tee 9 turn R at waymark into wood, follow well defined path to exit on to the golf course over footbridge, turn R along gravel track for 20m to waymark R. Follow fence R to gate, cross small meadow fence R to gate into Hammonds End Lane.

4 Turn R, go past Hammonds End House and farm R (S) with pond and barns L. Continue on the track which soon turns R, and in a few metres L (SW) with hedge and wood L. At the corner of the wood there is a seat (view to Redbournbury Mill), turn L along its boundary (SE). At the bottom of the field turn R (SW) passing three trees in the hedge L, (one dead). Path continues with hedge R, ignore other crossing paths to reach a crossing farm-access track.

5 Turn L along this track (SE) with trees R, towards the buildings in Redbournbury Farm. Turn R at signpost by river Ver and cross a footbridge, continue along N side of farm. In about 90m cross two more bridges over the River Ver to Redbournbury Mill R.

6 Turn sharp R before the signpost, go through mill forecourt and wooden gate (N) passing the mill R along a clear hedged track. Go through two gates, the field path continues (NW) with views of the river. This path bends (NW) and emerges on to the A5183 at a gate.

7 Cross the road to Dolittle Mill, go through a small gate and cross forecourt to small gate R, go through and continue (NW) with fence R and hedge L. At end of hedge and fence continue (N) along a clear path with hedge R to a gate. Go through gap then over bridge to Redbourn by-pass.

8 Cross this, turn L along Chequer Lane (W) passing the Nicky Line. Cross East Common and in a few metres turn R along a path past a children's play area to the old school. Opposite is the car park, the start of the walk.

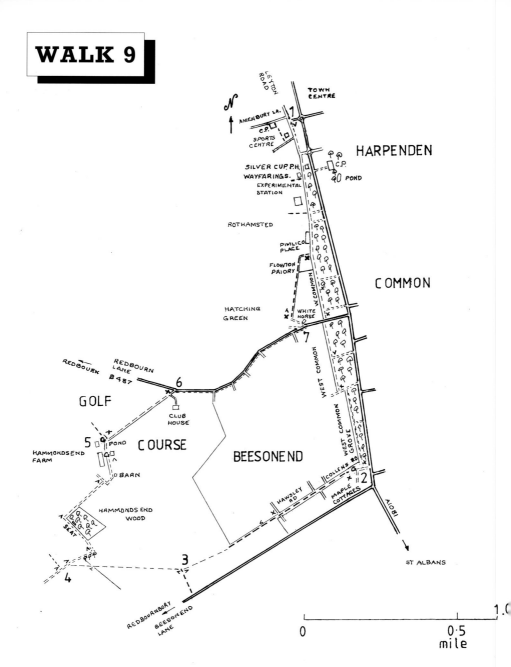

WALK 9

© Crown copyright

Total distance 5.2 miles (8.4km)

HARPENDEN AND HAMMONDS END

Park in public car park (parking fee) in Amenbury Lane, Harpenden.
G.R. 133,141 or on Harpenden Common G.R. 137,138.

1 From the car park, take the footpath (S) into Rothamsted Park. Turn L along the avenue of trees, go past the Sports Hall L, and out through the main entrance into Leyton Road. Turn R along this road (S). Continue into West Common noting the Rothamsted Laboratory R. Keep on past the attractive group of cottages called Pimlico Place R, and the extensive Flowton Priory. Cross Redbourn Lane and continue (S) along West Common. At the next road junction, a short L and R leads to West Common Grove. Notice the footpath parallel to this road just inside the tree line which you may prefer to use.

2 At the junction with a short access road leading to Maple Cottages, turn R and go past the end of the cottages L (SW). Go through the gate ahead into the Beesonend Estate. Continue (SW) along Collens Road into Hawsley Road, ignore transverse roads and enter a track that runs (SW) along the rear of housing. This clear path continues across a field (SW) and is much used. A waymark sign marks the junction of a path from Beesonend Lane.

3 Continue (W) along a clear track through a field, go through a gap in a crossing hedge at a waymark sign, and so downhill to a transverse track at another waymark.

4 Turn sharp R (NE) along this track with trees L. Continue with hedge R. The track turns sharp L along the boundary of Hammondsend Wood R, to a seat with views of Redbournbury Mill. Turn R (NE) along the northern boundary of the wood. At the next junction turn R, and in a few metres turn L passing a large barn R. Continue (N) past Hammonds End Farm and House L.

5 Turn R along the farm access road ignoring the gate L. This road passes the Golf Club House and leads to Redbourn Lane.

6 Turn R (E) along Redbourn Lane. There is a pleasant path on the R side of the road past some fine houses, leading to Hatching Green.

7 Here turn L along the lane (NW) at the White Horse P.H. R. At the end of the row of cottages is the junction with the access road to Rothamsted Manor. Here turn R along a pleasant gravel footpath (N) at the signpost. This meets West Common alongside the row of cottages in Pimlico Place, and so back to the car park.

WALK 10

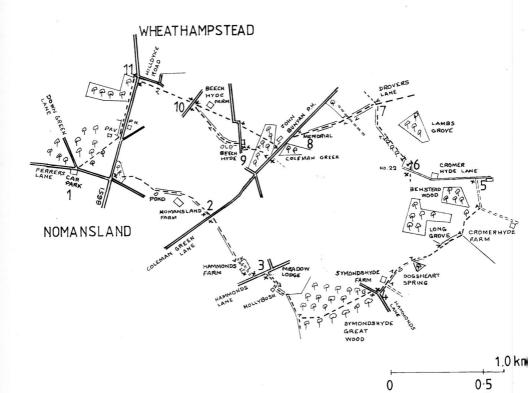

WHEATHAMPSTEAD

NOMANSLAND

© Crown copyright

Total distance 6.5 miles (10.5km)

NOMANSLAND, SYMONDSHYDE AND COLEMAN GREEN

WALK 10

Park in car park on Nomansland Common, at junction of Down Green Lane with Ferrers Lane. G.R. 171,124

1 Walk (E) along the common parallel with Ferrers Lane to the crossroads junction with B651. Take path (E) through small group of trees. This soon becomes a clear bridleway past Nomansland Farm R into Coleman Green Lane.

2 Cross this lane and continue (SE) along a clear bridleway into a farm track leading to Hammonds Farm. Go through the gateway, follow the signposts between farm buildings into the access road to Hammonds Lane. Turn L (NE) along this lane for about 100m.

3 Turn R (SE) into a gravel access road at Meadow Lodge and pass May Cottage R. At the entrance to Hollybush, turn L (E) along the boundary fence on a path to Symondshyde Great Wood. Turn R on to a clear path along the boundary fence of this wood (S). Continue under a power line to a junction with a waymarked track. Here turn sharp L (E) along a wide track which goes (NE) into Hammonds Lane at a gate.

4 Turn R (SE) along this lane and after a few metres turn L (NE) along the access road to Symondshyde Farm. Continue (NE) passing the farm and house L, into a meadow passing a small pond R. Continue (NE) with fence R to a small wood R called Dogsheart Spring. At this point proceed straight across the field to a waymarked hedge corner (NE). Continue with hedge L to waymark at hedge from R, then continue (N) across open field into the access road to Cromer Hyde Farm .Turn L along this track (N) into Cromer Hyde Lane.

5 Turn L along this lane (W) passing the cottages of Cromer Hyde, to a signpost opposite Cromer Hyde House.

6 Here turn R, through the large gate into the gravel entrance, go past the house L, to a stile just beyond a gate. Cross and continue diagonally (NW) across a small field to a double stile. Bear R across field to second oak tree. Continue (NW) alongside a raised bank and wire fence L to a stile. Cross and continue (NW) with hedge L downhill to a sunken lane called Drovers Lane.

7 Turn L along this lane (W) which crosses a transverse track and ends at the John Bunyan Chimney R.

8 At the junction with Coleman Green Lane, continue (SW) past the John Bunyan P H R. Take the track (SW) parallel with the road passing Coleman Green Cottages R. In about 100m is a waymark post. Turn R along a path through the trees (W). Ignore tracks leading off, continue (W) into a field. Cross this to a waymark post. Bear L along a garden fence into a crossing lane by a signpost, alongside Old Beech Hyde.

9 Turn R along this lane and in a few metres turn L into a wooded path (NW) opposite this house. This path opens into a headland path with hedge R and leads to a crossing lane alongside Beech Hyde Farm. Turn R at this lane and in a few metres turn L on to a field path opposite the gravel drive of this farm.

10 This clear path continues (NW) along a housing boundary fence R into Hilldyke Road at the junction with the Wheathampstead road B651.

11 Cross the road and take the footpath L (S). This path continues (S) parallel with the road and emerges on to Nomansland Common opposite the Wicked Lady PH. Here go (SW) through the Common to the car park at the junction of Ferrers and Down Green Lanes.

Alternatively at the John Bunyan PH item 8, take the path alongside Coleman Green Cottages (NW) through the woods. Continue (NW) straight across a field by a clear path into a lane at a bend. Go straight ahead along this lane. After about 40m at a sharp R bend, continue straight ahead along a clear track (NW) to Beech Hyde Farm into the poplar-lined access road of this farm. At the junction with the lane continue the walk from item 10, a slightly more direct route.

WALK 11

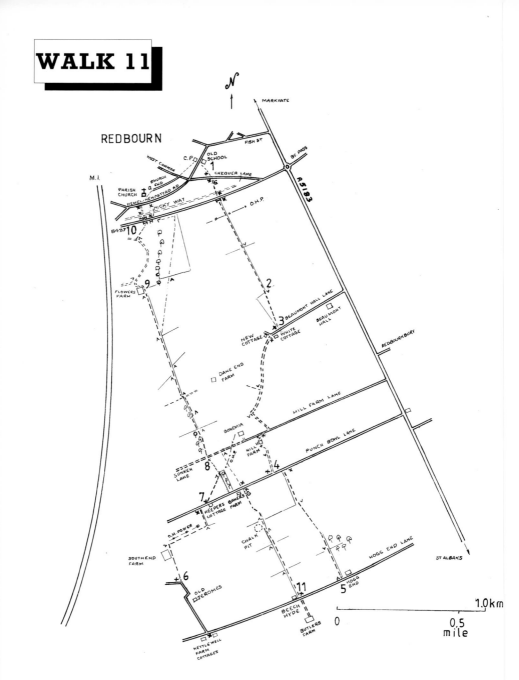

© Crown copyright

Total distance 5.5 miles (8.9km)
Shorter alternative 5.0 miles (8.1km)

REDBOURN TO HOGG END LANE

WALK 11

Park in public car park on Redbourn Common near the cricket pavilion opposite the old school. G.R. 103,119

1 Starting from the old school building now offices, take the path (S) around the children's play area. Cross Chequer Lane and River Red and continue (S) through a swing gate between housing. Cross the gravel track which is part of the 'Nicky Line' and the embankment using the steps. Cross the bypass to the signpost opposite and go up the steps to a stile. Cross this and continue (S) to a field corner where there is a waymark. Continue (S) through a gap in the hedge, with hedge L to the corner of the next field.

2 Here the definitive path veers R (S) across the next field to Beaumont Lane. Go up slope, head for tall trees at top right, until signpost in Beaumont Hall Lane comes into view.

3 Turn R along this lane, go past White Cottage L, after 70m bear L down a green lane passing New Cottage R. Ignore two paths R, this lane winds (SW) then (SE) to Hill Farm Lane, turn R along it to Hill Farm. Turn L (S) into the farm access road, then go R between farm buildings L and hay barn R to stile in fence R. Cross and turn L passing the farmhouse L, cross further stile to rejoin access road. Continue (S) to Punch Bowl Lane.

4 Turn L along this lane for about 90m, then at the signpost turn R. Follow the hedge R (S) to its end, then turn slightly L (SE) and cross an open field heading for a group of trees to R of the Abbey Tower seen in the distance, until waymark post is seen at end of hedge from R. Continue (S) along field track with hedge L to Hogg End Lane noting Hogg End Farm L.

5 Turn R (SW) along this lane, go past Butlers Farm L, on to Kettlewells Farm Cottages. Turn R along the lane signposted 'Old Jeromes', passing this house R.

6 Where the lane next turns sharp L, go through gap in hedge and continue ahead along a signposted farm track (N) passing Southend Farm L. At the farm boundary, turn R across a field (NE) parallel to the power line L. At the hedge turn L (NW) to Punch Bowl Lane.

7 Turn R along lane for about 50m to signpost L just before Keepers Cottage. Enter field and cross diagonally (NE) to corner of a small wood. Walk downhill (N) to waymark post in hedge gap and enter sunken lane.

8 Cross this lane to the waymark opposite and follow (N) through the line of trees ahead to a waymark at hedge. The path goes (N) with hedge R then after 120m crosses over to hedge L by spinney R. At a four-way path junction, with Dane End Farm in a (NE) direction, the path transfers and continues with hedge R (N). After 150m go through hedge gap and continue with hedge R towards Flowers Farm.

9 At Flowers Farm go along the access road (N) with farm buildings L, turn R downhill at T-junction with waymark. As road curves (W) at waymark at end of hedge R, bear R across corner of field to a stile. Cross this and stile opposite, go down steps and cross the by-pass. Go up the steps opposite over embankment.

10 Cross the 'Nicky Line' gravel path, go along a short lane (N) to the Hemel Hempstead Road, and turn R to Redbourn Parish Church. Cross into the churchyard (NE) to the gateway in Church End, noting the old cottages and Hollybush PH. Continue (E), cross West Common Road and so to the car park ahead R.

Alternatively a slightly shorter walk can be devised at item 5. In Hogg End Lane turn R (N) opposite Butlers Farm alongside Beech Hyde. This track goes (N) with hedge L to a waymark and continues (N) across field to waymark in hedge in next field. Continue (N) with hedge L to waymark where hedge crosses over to become hedge R. Continue to an old chalk pit. Ahead is a whitewashed house called Bakers Farm. The path crosses an open field (N) passing this house L to a pipe gateway and signpost in Punch Bowl Lane. Cross to the signpost opposite, continue (N) towards power poles and waymark near corner of fenced paddock R. Continue a short distance (N) parallel to fence R to waymark at gap in hedge ahead and into sunken lane. Then turn L (W) along lane to reach waymark at item 8.

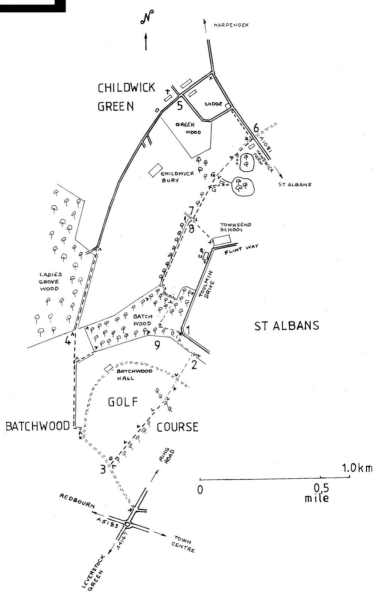

N

HARPENDEN

CHILDWICK
GREEN

5

LODGE

GREEN
WOOD

6 A1081

HARWICK
FARM

ST ALBANS

CHILDWICK
BURY

7

8

TOWNSEND
SCHOOL

FLINT WAY

TOULMIN
DRIVE

LADIES
GROVE
WOOD

BATCH
WOOD

1

ST ALBANS

4

9

2

BATCHWOOD
HALL

GOLF

BATCHWOOD

COURSE

RING
ROAD

3

REDBOURN

A5183

TOWN
CENTRE

A4147

LEVERSTOCK
GREEN

1.0 km

0   0,5
           mile

© Crown copyright

Total distance 4.2 miles (6.8km)

30

BATCHWOOD AND CHILDWICK GREEN

Park in recreation ground car park G.R. 143,150 or discreetly in Toulmin Drive, St. Albans adjacent to BatchWood. G.R. 141,092

1 Walk (S) down Toulmin Drive with Batchwood (R), and where the road turns sharp L at number 18, continue (S) along a bridleway with woods R. At a crossing chain-link fence, turn L, keeping this fence R.

2 At a wide waymarked gap in this fence, turn R, and continue (SW) across the golf course. The route is liberally marked with waymark signs. Cross the Batchwood Hall access road, go through a narrow belt of trees and continue (SW) with belt of trees L to the access road by a waymark post and gate.

3 Turn R along this road and in 250m turn L at a signposted bridleway. This soon turns R (N) with a hedge R along the boundary of the golf course. Ignore the path R, and continue along this well used path across a field to the corner of Ladies Grove Wood.

4 Continue (N) along a fenced path alongside the edge of the wood, into the access road which passes the large house Childwickbury, and leads to the hamlet of Childwick Green.

5 Near the pump turn R (SE) along a road lined with rhododendron bushes. The road bends L and meets the St. Albans to Harpenden road by Childwick Lodge. Turn R and walk along the footpath/cycle path (SE) alongside the road for about 300m to Hawswick Farm.

6 Turn R at the farm entrance along the gravel track (SW) to the end of the pine wood L. Ignore paths going L and straight ahead, bear R to a wooden gate in the corner of the field. Go through the gate along a wide fenced track between hedges (SW). Go through the large iron gate and continue (SW) to emerge from a narrow belt of trees.

7 Here a bridleway follows the hedge L (SE) and sports field R into Toulmin Drive along which you reach the start of the walk.

8 **Alternatively** a more interesting route from item 7 is to continue (SW) alongside a belt of trees R with an open field L. Follow the headland path past a pond R, bear L to a large gap in the corner of the wood where the tree line runs N. At this corner a small waymarked path runs (SW) into the wood for about 200m to a crossing path by a large oak tree with waymarks. Here turn L for a further 200m through the wood to the start in Toulmin Drive.

Note: There is now a permissive path around Batch Wood indicated by posts with white arrows.

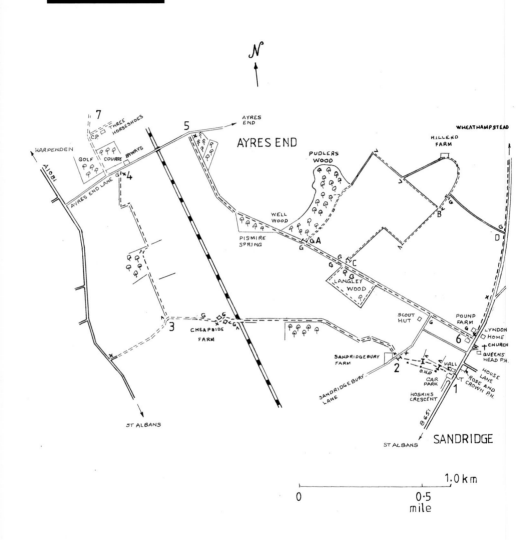

N

© Crown copyright

Total distance 4.3 miles (6.8km) or from Three Horseshoes 4.5 miles (7.2km)

SANDRIDGE AND AYRES END

Park in public car park in Sandridge by the Village Hall,
where there are toilets and a public telephone. G.R. 169,104

1 From the car park go past children's play area along the fence R of the recreation ground (W) to a stile. Cross stile and follow the power line (W) to a second stile and continue to a third signposted stile in Sandridgebury Lane.

2 Immediately opposite at another signpost, the path continues (W) between fences or hedges past a small plantation L. A short length with hedges on both sides leads to a brick bridge over the railway. Cross this and go through the wooden gate. Look for a farm gate ahead (NW) alongside a group of farm buildings L. Go through this gate and the farmyard, and on to the access road of Cheapside Farm opposite a signpost. Turn R along this road (W) and go through another gate. In about 400m where the road turns L there is a track R.

3 Turn R and go along this track (N) with hedge L. Continue past new tree plantation L with hedge R, to a crossing hedge at the bottom. Bear R with hedge L for a few metres, then turn L through a gap in this hedge. Continue (N) with hedge L, into Ayres End Lane by a gate.

4 Turn R along this road, passing a house called 'Byways' and go over the railway bridge. In a further 300m, the road bears R and a track goes sharp R by a large felled tree trunk at a signpost.

5 This track continues (S) then (SE) past small areas of woodland. Unless taking alternative options 8, ignore transverse tracks at point A, Well Wood and point C, Langley Wood, and continue (SE) past the Scout Hut R. This leads through Pound Farm to Sandridge High Street (B651).

6 Here turn R, noting the Queen's Head PH L. The Parish Church of St. Leonard is worth a visit. Continue (SW) along Sandridge High Street to the Village Hall car park. There are a number of public houses in Sandridge where refreshment is available.

7 **Alternatively** it is possible to park near the Three Horseshoes PH on Harpenden Golf Course G.R.143,120. Then from item 4 one may continue to Sandridge returning via items 1,2 3 and 4 to the car park.

8 **Alternatively** : The walk can be extended along permissive paths from points A or C. The paths enjoy good views. All options add approximately 1 mile to the walk.

OPTIONS A,D and C,B,D. When reaching point D, turn R and follow the footpath along the field edge inside the fence towards Sandridge , to item 6 Pound Farm

OPTION A,B,C. When reaching point C, turn L and follow text from item 5 Langley Wood

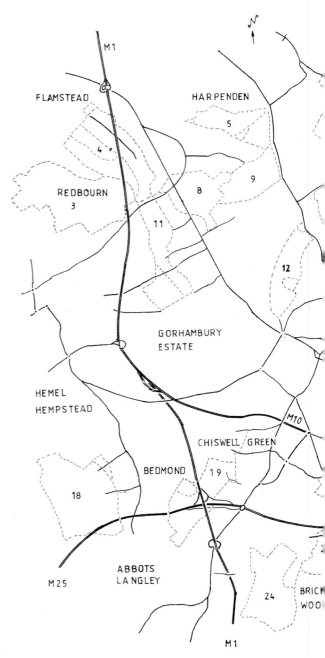

© Crown copyright

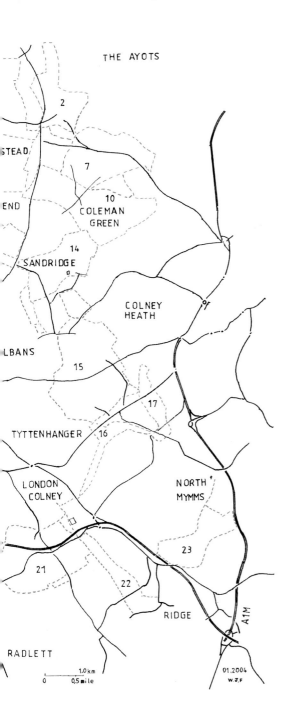

THE AYOTS

2

STEAD

END

7

10
COLEMAN
GREEN

14
SANDRIDGE

COLNEY
HEATH

LBANS

15

17

TYTTENHANGER   16

LONDON
COLNEY

NORTH
MYMMS

23

21

22

RIDGE

A1M

RADLETT

1.0 km
0   0.5 mile

01.2004
W.J.F

24 FOOTPATH
WALKS AROUND
ST ALBANS

35

WALK 14

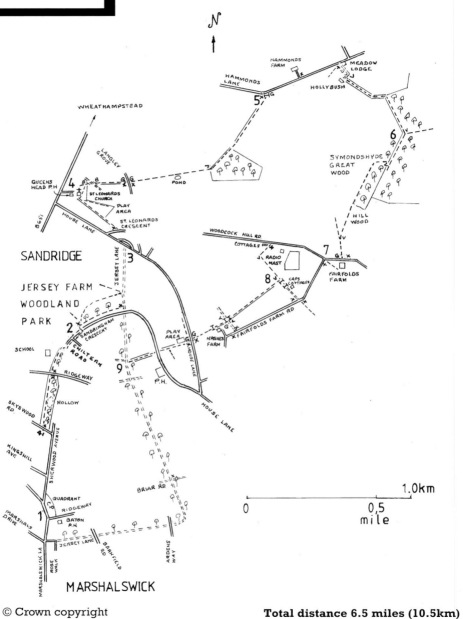

N

WHEATHAMPSTEAD

HAMMONDS FARM

MEADOW LODGE

HAMMONDS LANE

HOLLYBUSH

5

LANGLEY GROVE

SYMONDSHYDE GREAT WOOD

QUEENS HEAD P.H

4

ST. LEONARDS CHURCH

PLAY AREA

POND

6

HILL WOOD

B651

HOUSE LANE

ST. LEONARDS CRESCENT

WOODCOCK HILL RD.

COTTAGES

SANDRIDGE

RADIO MAST

7

FAIRFOLDS FARM

JERSEY LANE

3

8

CAPS COTTAGES

JERSEY FARM

WOODLAND

PARK

2

SANDRINGHAM CRESCENT

PLAY AREA

NASHES FARM

FAIRFOLDS FARM RD.

SCHOOL

CHILTERN ROAD

9

HOUSE LANE

RIDGEWAY

P.H.

SKYSWOOD RD.

HOLLOW

HOUSE LANE

4

KINGSHILL AVE

SHERWOOD AVENUE

BRIAR RD.

QUADRANT

RIDGEWAY

MARSHALS DRIVE

1

BATON P.H.

ARDENS WAY

MARSHALSWICK LA.

JERSEY LANE

BANFIELD

ROSE WALK

MARSHALSWICK

1.0km

0   0.5
        mile

© Crown copyright

Total distance 6.5 miles (10.5km)

MARSHALSWICK, SANDRIDGE AND SYMONDSHYDE

**Park in public car park at the Quadrant, Marshalswick, St. Albans.
G.R. 169,086. Public toilets are available near the library in The Ridgeway.**

1 Go past the shops R along Sherwood Avenue (N) and pass Kingshill Avenue. At the next turning, Skyswood Road, turn L and in a few metres alongside number 41, turn R along a footpath through a small wood (N). Keep to the fence L, pass a small hollow R and cross the transverse road, The Ridgeway. Continue (N) along a wooded path by the boundary fence of school L.

2 This path emerges on to a road junction. Use the crossing and keep L for 50m, using a crossing refuge in Sandringham Crescent cross the road to signposted path (NE,) a wooded path with housing R parallel with the road. In about 400m is a crossing asphalt track called Jersey Lane, turn L (N). **Alternatively** Enter the woodland park and follow an open path bearing R (NE) downhill, which also meets Jersey Lane, turn L (N). Ignore other footpaths and continue along Jersey Lane to its junction with House Lane.

3 Turn L along this road and take the next turning R called St. Leonards Crescent (NE). A few metres along this is a footpath L at a signpost. This goes along a boundary fence, past a small play area then a cemetery to the Parish Church of St. Leonard which is worth a visit.

4 Take the path R (N) along the east end of the church to the (NE) corner of the churchyard. Cross the asphalt lane at the pipe rail barriers, and turn R (E) along a track with garages L and a hedge R. Cross Langley Grove into a wide grassy track opposite (E). Continue on across open fields, past a small pond R, then enter a small wood. Continue (NE) with the boundary of the wood L. On emerging from the wood, the path follows the headland with a ditch and hedge L.

5 Cross the stile into Hammonds Lane, turn R go past Hammonds Farm L. After a further 150m turn R (SE) into a gravel track at Meadow Lodge. Follow this along to the house called Hollybush then turn L (E) along the boundary fence between hedges on a path to Symondshyde Great Wood. Turn R at the corner of the wood (S) into a clear path inside the boundary fence of the wood R (S).

6 At waymark post, ignore the track L and continue (S) along a broad track through the woods. In about 200m the track turns R at a waymark. In a further 50m turn L (SW) inside the edge of the wood. This emerges on to a grassy track (S) leading to Fairfolds Farm. Go through the gate and turn R (W) along the road.

7 At the fork in the road turn L (S) passing the radio mast and buildings R. Soon turn R (NW) on to a private road which is a public right of way leading to Cap's Cottages R. Cross two stiles ahead with boundary fence R, and turn L immediately after the second stile. **Alternatively** at the fork in the road turn R and proceed (NW) along Woodcock Hill Road passing the radio mast L. At Woodcock Hill Cottages turn L at the signpost, then L again along the boundary fence to a stile where you turn R (SW) without crossing the stile.

8 Continue downhill (SW) with barbed wire fence L to a gap on to a transverse track with stile opposite. Cross this into the field passing Nashes Farm L (SW) to another stile with fence L. Keep on downhill, bear L, go through gate, cross House Lane with care, go through a second gate and cross a gravel track. Keep straight ahead with hedge L and childs play area R. The path continues (SW) and soon becomes asphalt surfaced between housing. Cross the next road and soon meet a transverse track. This is Jersey Lane. Turn L (S).

9 This lane continues (S) between housing, crosses a bridleway and eventually turns R crossing Ardens Way and Barnfield Road. Just before crossing Rose Walk the lane becomes an asphalt surfaced access road. Go on ahead to meet Marshalswick Lane at the junction with Marshals Drive. Turn R (N) along this road, cross the Ridgeway and so return to the Quadrant car park. Here the shops are worth attention, and refreshments are available at the garage.

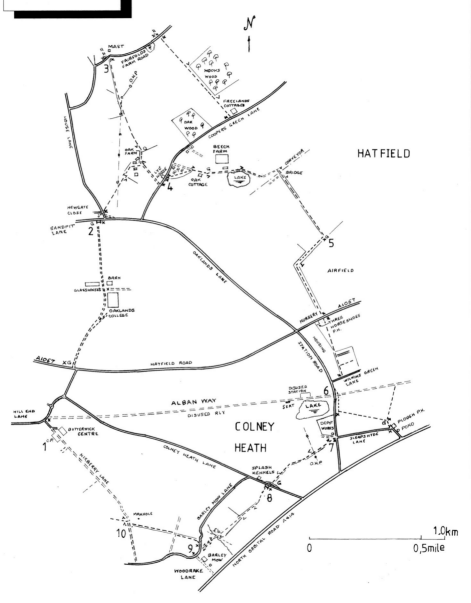

WALK 15

© Crown copyright

Total distance 7.3 miles (11.8km) or by alternative Alban Way 6.2 miles (10km)

OAKLANDS, SMALLFORD AND SLEAPSHYDE

WALK
15

Park discreetly in Hixberry Lane near junction with Hill End Lane. G.R. 179,069

1 Return past the Butterwick Day Centre R, turn R into Hill End Lane (N), then L along Colney Heath Lane. Turn L into Hatfield Road, and cross to the main entrance gate of Oaklands College. Continue (N) along this pleasant drive, ignore a R fork. The drive bears L past the college R and soon continues as a wide gravel track (N) and meets Sandpit Lane.

2 Cross the road into the asphalt path opposite (NE) and in a few metres is the junction of Newgate Close with House Lane. Cross the lane to a signpost opposite this junction. Go through the gap in the hedge, and continue (NE) across a field. Go uphill (NE) past a power line post L, cross a stile towards Oak Farm. Go through gates between two large barns ahead, past the farmhouse L to the access road. Turn R over stile then turn L (N) along a clear track and pass the farm L. Continue (N) passing under the power line. Note the masts ahead and with wire fence L, meet Fairfolds Farm Road.

3 Turn R along the road (NE) to a signpost R opposite a private road entrance. Turn R (SE) across a field on a clear path noting a large wood ahead. The path meets the boundary of Hooks Wood L. At the far corner of this wood, continue across a field passing Freelands Cottages L, to a signpost in the hedge bordering Coopers Green Lane. Turn R along this lane (SW) passing Oak Wood R. Pass the entrances to Beech Farm drive L, and after a few metres in a small copse, is a stile L.

4 Cross this stile, and go through this copse (NE) to a transverse access road. Turn R (E) pass Oak Cottage R, and just before the gate to Beech Farm, bear R along a fence past the farm L and with quarry infill lake R, to join a wide access track running (SE) which crosses a conveyor belt at a small bridge. Go straight ahead along a wide path (SE) to the airfield boundary fence.

5 Turn sharp R at the gate and signpost (SW), continue with hedge and fence L. Turn L between chain link fences (SE) into Hatfield Road at the Nursery. Cross the road to a signpost and stile opposite noting the Three Horseshoes PH, and continue (SE) with housing R. This clear path emerges on to Wilkins Green Lane where turn R to Station Road.

6 Turn L (S) along an asphalt path which slopes down to cross the Alban Way track. Continue (S) along a path with hedge R parallel with the road. At the next signpost turn L along a firm asphalt track (SE) across a field. At the junction of paths turn R to the Plough PH in the hamlet of Sleapshyde. Turn R along Sleapshyde Lane (W). At the junction with Station Road cross to the stile with signpost.

7 Cross this stile to a clear path over Colney Heath (SW). Follow a random spaced hedge L, cross under the power line and keeping hedge L continue parallel to the A414, to a waymarked kissing gate, go through, turn R and continue into Colney Heath Lane.

8 Immediately opposite is a signpost and stile. Cross and go (SW) across a field to a hedge. Go round the hedge, and continue with hedge R (SW) to a three way hedge junction. The path now goes diagonally across the field with hedge L eventually meeting a small hidden stream. Cross the small footbridge in a hedge and continue (SW) between fences and over stiles into the lane.

9 Turn R along Barley Mow Lane (N) and in about 40m turn L (W) at signpost just before the lane turns R. A clear path follows a hedge and ditch R (W). At a transverse track, turn R and then L along a path with hedge and ditch L (W). This leads to a transverse lane, turn R at the waymark post. This is Hixberry Lane,

10 Turn R along this lane to the car park.

Alternatively at item 6 go down to the old railway line called the Alban Way, turn R (W) along this pleasant track to Hill End Lane. Turn L to the car park.

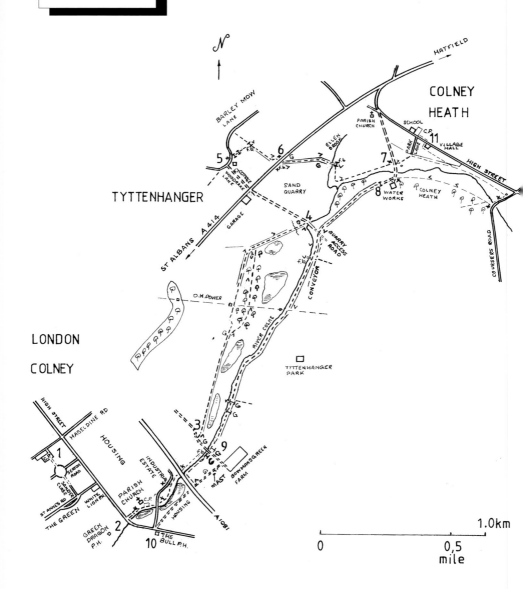

© Crown copyright

Total distance 6.5 miles (10.5km) o
by the alternative route 5.5 miles
(8.9km) Using the car park by St.
Peters Church 5.6 miles (9km)

LONDON COLNEY, RIVER COLNE AND COLNEY HEATH

Park in public car park in Haseldine Road, London Colney, G.R. 177,041 or in car park by St. Peters Church G.R. 182,037 at item 2.

NOTE:- The A414 has to be crossed twice, there are safe central reservations.

1 Take the asphalt path between housing at rear of car park (SE), go through a circle of housing to path opposite (SE) which leads into Sanders Close. At The Green, turn L along St. Annes Road (NE). At White Lion PH turn R into High Street and continue (SE) towards the river. Just before reaching the bridge, turn L past St Peter's Church

2 A gravel track now follows the river bank (NE). Cross the access road leading to the industrial estate. The track meets another access road in 150 metres, then continues (NE) along the river bank R. Ignore footbridge R and go under the A1081 road bridge. At the far side continue (NE) along the river bank to the farm access road.

3 Turn L and in a few metres take the second R turn (N) along a track with hedge or fence R. Head for the power line pylon, noting the lakes in the old quarry infill R. Continue (N) and where the track turns L, bear R into a new plantation. Go through the woodland keeping to the lefthand path, under the pylon cables. Continue through new woodland, ignore path and car park L, continue straight ahead and when this path meets an access track, bear R (NE). Go past the drainage pond R to an iron gate L at Tyttenhanger Quarry works.

4 Go through gate, turn L and go along concrete access road (NW) with care to the A414. Cross A414 into a narrow asphalt lane opposite, marked by iron posts. Continue (NW) past Woodrake Cottage into Barley Mow Lane.

5 At this junction turn R (NE) at the signpost into a path between fences. Cross the stiles to a small footbridge into a field, immediately turn R (SE). Cross a footbridge over a small ditch and continue (SE) with hedge and stream R. This bends L and runs parallel to the A414, then in 75 metres turn R through trees to a signpost on the A414. Cross the road to a small footbridge opposite.

6 Cross this bridge, go through a metal gate and continue ahead (E) on a fenced path between lakes, through a second gate and turn half R. This leads to a footbridge over the Ellen Brook. Cross the bridge and stile, continue with river R (S) and open field L. The path bears L (E) along the bank of the river Colne through a metal barrier into Church Lane. Cross over on to Colney Heath near coal post.

7 Continue (E) across the Heath with housing L and the river R to another coal post near the Cock PH. Turn R and cross the river by the bridge in Coursers Road. Turn R again at the signpost and go (W) across the Heath with river R and woodland L. This pleasant path follows the river to the Water Works access road. Turn L along this road, go past the Water Works L and a group of houses R (SW).

8 Continue along a track with Works L, then after about 100m cross a metal stile into a field path with hedge R (SW). In about 500m is a large steel bridge R used by quarry vehicles. Cross the quarry access road and the conveyor belt ahead. Bear L (S) on to a bridleway, continue with river R and wire fence L, heading for the power pylon. At the pylon turn sharp R then L. The path now follows the river bank for about 1km passing Tyttenhanger Park L.

9 The path leads to Willows Farm Village L. Continue (SW) over stiles and gates along a fenced path to the farm concrete access road. Cross, go through a gate along a fenced track, turn L at A1081 embankment and proceed to the farm access road. Turn R, go under the A1081 road bridge. Continue (SW) along a road with housing L, lakes and river R, to the High Street opposite the Bull PH.

10 Turn R along the High Street, cross the river by the so-called Telfords Bridge. Note the picturesque Waterside L. Continue past the White Lion PH (NW) and return to Haseldine Road. Turn L for the car park.

11 **Alternatively:** This walk can be started from Colney Heath. Park in public car park next to Colney Heath School G.R. 201,061. From here cross the road, turn L along the High Street to the village hall. Turn R then L along the Heath with river R. Cross the road at Coursers Road bridge and continue to items 8,9, 10. At item 10 cross the ridge to item 2 if you do not wish to visit London Colney. Continue then to item 7. At the coal post go (E) across the Heath for about 50m into Park Lane. This leads to the High Street opposite the car park.

41

WALK 17

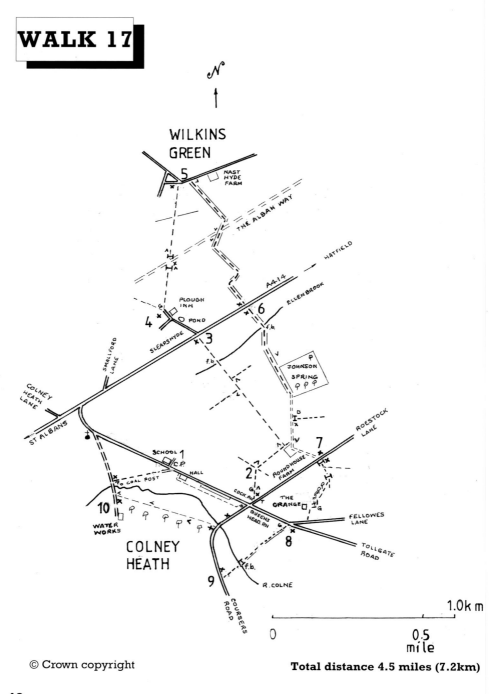

WILKINS GREEN

5

NAST HYDE FARM

THE ALBAN WAY

HATFIELD

A414

ELLENBROOK

PLOUGH INN

POND

4

6

f.b.

SLEAPSHYDE

3

f.b.

JOHNSON SPRING

SMALLFORD LANE

COLNEY HEATH LANE

ST ALBANS

ROESTOCK LANE

7

SCHOOL
C.P.

1

HALL

2

ROUNDHOUSE FARM

TO COAL POST

COCK P.H.

THE GRANGE

FELLOWES LANE

10

QUEENS HEAD P.H.

8

WATER WORKS

TOLLGATE ROAD

COLNEY HEATH

9

f.b.

R. COLNE

COURSERS ROAD

1.0 km

0   0.5
                                   mile

© Crown copyright

Total distance 4.5 miles (7.2km)

COLNEY HEATH AND WILKINS GREEN

Park in public car park next to Colney Heath School.
G.R. 201,061

NOTE:- The A414 has to be crossed twice, there are safe central reservations.

1 From the car park turn L along the High Street (SE) passing Scholars Court R. Turn R at Village Hall, then L along grassy track parallel with road (SE). Continue along rear of housing to large white coal post, rejoin road near crossroads. Cross and turn L at the Queens Head PH along Roestock Lane for a few metres, to a signposted gap between housing. Go L (N) through this and a gate to a gap between metal posts at a junction of power lines. Take the clear path (N) diagonally across the field.

2 At a clear crossing of paths turn half R and continue (NE) across a field. Soon is a hedge R then a junction of bridleways at a waymark post. Here turn sharp L (NW) along a gravel track with ditch R. Soon this track becomes fenced on both sides, continue ahead ignoring all paths off the main track, cross a bridge over a stream and carry on to the A414.

3 At the junction with the A414, cross with care to Sleapshyde Lane. Continue through Sleapshyde to the Plough PH R. Go through the gap at the side of an iron gate (N).

4 Here ignore the path L, instead take the path half R (N) across the field, This crosses the 'Alban Way' and continues (N) across another field to Wilkins Green.

5 Turn R along the lane (E) and after a few metres turn R into a hedged bridleway (SE). Recross the 'Alban Way' and continue to the A414. This path may be muddy in wet weather.

6 Cross over and continue (SE). Go past a wood L, at the southern corner the track becomes a gravel road which passes Roundhouse Farm, and meets Roestock Lane at Cherry Green Trees.

7 Cross the road, and the stile opposite (S) to another stile at the edge of trees. Turn half R across the playing field, along a row of trees. Go through an iron gate, continue ahead to a T-junction opposite The Grange, turn L and in a few metres turn R into Fellowes Lane. Turn R along this to the junction with Tollgate Road, and cross to the stile opposite.

8 Continue (SW) along a clear path with hedge L over a stile. Cross the river Colne at the footbridge, and then between wood L and fence R into Coursers Road.

9 Turn R (N) along the road and at the bend turn L (NW) at a waymark sign. This pleasant path across the Heath with the river R and trees L meets an access road.

10 Turn R (N) noting the coal post on the right, cross the Colne river and immediately turn R again (E) on a path through trees leading to housing and the High Street. Cross over to the car park L.

WALK 18

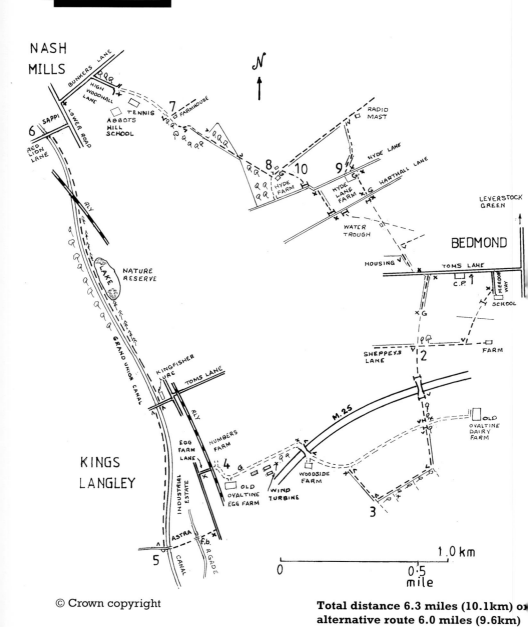

© Crown copyright

Total distance 6.3 miles (10.1km) or alternative route 6.0 miles (9.6km)

44

BEDMOND, GRAND UNION CANAL AND NASH MILLS

Park in Recreation Area, Playing Fields,
Toms Lane, Bedmond. G.R. 095,035.

1 From the car park, turn L down Toms Lane. At the signpost by number 190, turn L (S) into a path with fence R and hedge L. Go through a gate and across a field to a waymark in Sheppeys Lane.

2 Cross this track, continue (S) over another field to a footbridge over the M25 which has a stile at each end. Continue forward (S) crossing the farm access road, to another crossing path. Turn R (SW) along this path along the boundary of housing L with a field R.

3 At the next crossing path turn R (NW). This path with fence L meets the same access road crossed in item 2. Bear L along this road passing on L a farmhouse 'Woodside' to a vehicle bridge over the M25 again. Continue along this road (W) passing a wind turbine and the old Ovaltine Egg Farm L, carry on downhill.

4 Turn L (SW) under the railway bridge where a short road leads to a T-junction with the Kings Langley road. Turn L (SE) along this road passing an industrial trading estate R. At the boundary of this estate, turn R along a fenced path (SW). Cross the river Gade by the bridge, continue along the boundary fence, and cross the canal by a second bridge.

5 Turn L down steps and L again under the bridge and along the towpath (N). Follow the Grand Union waymarks on to the next bridge in Toms Lane, cross over the canal, turn R down steps and R again under bridge on to towpath (N) passing the housing Kingfisher Lure. This pleasant path continues (N) past a lake, and under the railway bridge to Red Lion Lane.

6 Here a Grand Union waymark points L, do not follow this but take an unsigned clear path ahead to Red Lion Lane, turn R in this Lane (NE). At the junction with Lower Road turn L (N) towards Nash Mill. (SAPPI). Take the next turning R (NE) which is Bunkers Lane by a flint wall R. Take the next turning R, High Woodhall Lane. Go past Abbot's Hill School entrance R, and continue along an access road uphill (SE) past Tennis Academy, this eventually leads to a large farmhouse. Ignore the track L, instead turn R into a small copse.

7 This path continues (SE) along the boundary of the farmhouse through the copse to a waymark. Bear L as indicated, continue downhill alongside a hedge R (SE). At foot of hill look for waymark L in woodland fence and continue(SE) uphill through wood into a field path with hedge R leading to Hyde Farm

8 Do not enter the farm, turn L along a clear track past a metal barn L. This soon becomes a field path with hedge R leading to a radio mast (NE). Turn R at the waymark about 200m before reaching the mast along a headland path then a fenced track (SE), into Hyde Lane.

9 Turn L in this lane, and in a few metres turn R through a gate along the side of Hyde Lane Farm. This fenced path leads (SE) through a gate into Harthall Lane. Cross the lane to stile and field path (SE). This leads to a water trough at the intersection of two paths. Continue (SE) to a gap in hedge, continue with hedge L. A fenced path continues (SE) along the boundary of housing R to a gap in Toms Lane. Turn L up Toms Lane to the car park R.

10 **Alternatively** at item 8 turn R at the metal barn, go through a swing gate into a field. Continue (SE) to a stile in the hedge corner and cross into Hyde Lane. Go L along this lane for a few metres, turn R at a signposted track with hedge L (SE) into Harthall Lane. Turn L, in a few metres turn R and cross a stile where path leads to the water trough in item 9.

WALK 19

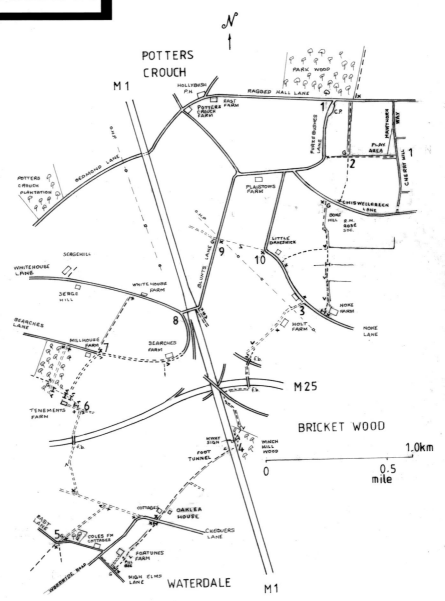

© Crown copyright

Total distance 6.8 miles (11.0km)
Slightly shorter by the alternative
route

POTTERS CROUCH AND
MOTORWAY INTERCHANGE

**Parking is available on E side of Furzebushes Lane near junction with
Ragged Hall Lane G.R. 127.051. Also limited parking is possible
in Cherry Hill, Chiswell Green by the children's recreation ground G.R.131,049**

1 FURZEBUSHES LANE START. Turn R (E) along Ragged Hall Lane for about 50m. Then turn R (S) through a gate along a fenced path to a gate at a transverse path Item 2.
CHERRY HILL START. Go through the gate adjacent to the children's recreation area on a path between fences. This continues (W) with fence R to a small gate R, here turn L Item 2.

2 Continue (S) across a well defined path towards woodlands and a signpost opposite Bone Hill, the R.N.Rose Society. Turn R along Chiswell Green Lane for 50m. Turn L (S) at the signpost and metal gate, and go along the boundary fence left of Bone Hill. At the waymark continue ahead (S) and cross the stile in the hedge. Continue (S) into a farm track with hedge L towards Noke Farm. Bear R (SW) in front of this farm L, to a stile and signpost in Noke Lane. Turn R along this lane, and after 100m at a R bend, turn L along a bridleway marked 'Private Road'.

3 This track passes Holt Farm L and continues (SW), in 60m after path turns R between fields, turn L at a waymark post. Aim (S) at a gap in trees to reach a motorway bridge over an M25 feeder road. Continue (S) down steps to a second bridge over the M25 where there is a good view of the M25/M1 interchange. The path continues R between chain link fences and goes under another feeder road bridge. At the end of the fencing turn R, continue (S) through Winch Hill Wood to the M1 boundary fence. Cross the stile near the motorway sign, go down the steps to a foot tunnel under the M1.

4 On emerging from the tunnel, continue (SW) along a clear path with hedge L. Ignore a track L, and continue to Chequers Lane at Oaklea House L. Cross the lane to a signposted stile. Continue uphill fence R (SW) passing Fortunes Farm R. Go past the pill box R (SW) to a stile in High Elms Lane. Then turn R along the asphalt track parallel with the lane. At the junction turn R along Chequers Lane. In a few metres turn L (W) into East Lane past Coles Farm Cottages.

5 The lane turns sharp L then R. At the signpost, go sharp R through a gate into a bridleway (NE) with small copse R. In about 350m at a transverse bridleway turn L (W) at a signpost. At the next signposted fork bear R (N) uphill along a gravel bridleway leading to a vehicle bridge over the M25. Cross this continue (N) to a crossing track leading to Tenements Farm L.

6 Do not enter the farm, look for a waymarked stile R and cross into a meadow. Turn L (NW) keep to a hedge L and in 150 metres cross a stile into the farm access road. Another stile opposite leads to a pleasant meadow with woods ahead. Continue (NW) between two large oaks with belt of trees L, go up the slope to a stile in the trees not easily seen. Cross and go straight ahead along a wide track in the woods (N). This meets Searches Lane along which turn R (E) to Millhouse Farm.

7 Continue (E) along this lane now only a grassy track. Go past Searches Farm L, into the access road adjacent to the motorway R to the bridge in Blunts Lane.
Alternatively in wet weather at the signpost opposite Millhouse Farm, take the gravel track (NE) with hedge L into Whitehouse Lane. Turn R past Whitehouse Farm L to the bridge in Blunts Lane.

8 Turn R over the bridge across the many feeder lanes at this junction. Continue (NE) along this lane to the overhead power line.

9 Turn R (E) at the signpost along a grass path, across a field to a signpost just to L of a large house in Noke Lane.

10 Turn L (NE) in this lane uphill to next junction, bear R then L into Furzebushes Lane, when the road turns sharp L take the footpath R (E) alongside a fence L to the start at Cherry Hill. **OR** continue along the lane to car park at Furzebushes Lane.

WALK 20

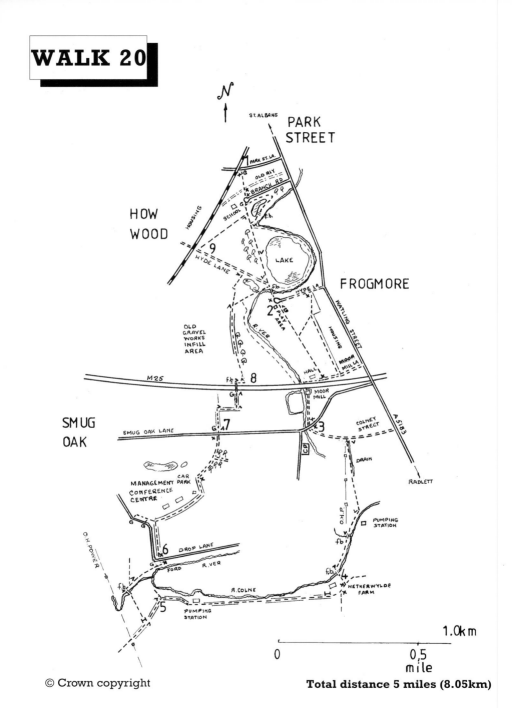

N

ST. ALBANS

PARK STREET

PARK ST. LA.

OLD RLY

BRANCH RD

SCHOOL

HOW WOOD

HOUSING

HYDE LANE

9

LAKE

FROGMORE

HYDE LA.

WATLING STREET

2

PLAY AREA

HOUSING

OLD GRAVEL WORKS INFILL AREA

R. VER

MOOR LA.

M25

fb

8

HALL

MOOR MILL

SMUG OAK

SMUG OAK LANE

G 7

3

COLNEY STREET

A 5183

CP

DRAIN

RADLETT

MANAGEMENT CONFERENCE CENTRE

CAR PARK

O.H.P.

PUMPING STATION

O.H. POWER

6

DROP LANE

G

FORD

R. VER

fb

O.H.P.

fb

4

NETHERWYLDE FARM

fb

R. COLNE

5

PUMPING STATION

1.0 km

0   0,5
                    mile

© Crown copyright

Total distance 5 miles (8.05km)

48

PARK STREET, RIVERS VER AND COLNE

WALK 20

Park in Park Street Lane, Park Street, near playing field. G.R. 147,038

1 Enter the playing field at the gate near the railway bridge, take the asphalt path, passing the children's play area R (SE). Go through the gap in the old disused railway, cross Branch Road and pass the school entrance R. Go through the gate opposite into the wide gravel track (S). Here a small diversion is worth trying. Immediately turn L, with lake R on a path which meets the river Ver (E). Turn R between the river and the lake, cross a small stream by the footbridge then the path rejoins the original gravel track. Turn L along this track continue (SE) passing a plantation R. The track goes between two lakes, passes waymarked posts R and crosses the river by a footbridge into a parking area at the end of Hyde Lane.

2 Go straight ahead (SE) up steps through gate across the infill area. Emerge through an iron gate into Moor Mill Lane near the river. Turn R on to the gravel track between fences at the signpost near Building Supplies yard. Continue under the motorway bridge along the river bank to Moor Mill. The path continues with a short L and R round the mill into the access road to Smug Oak Lane.

3 Cross Smug Oak Lane into the bridleway opposite at the signpost. Take this gravel track (E) and in 150m turn R through a waymarked gap. Continue and go due (S) with power line R. This continues with a drain L and the pumping station ahead. At the bank of the river turn R along it. At a power line post carrying a junction of wires is a footbridge. Cross this and continue with river L towards the group of buildings Netherwylde Farm. Before reaching the farm turn L crossing a bridge over the river Colne.

4 Go through a small copse R to the signpost on a transverse bridleway. Turn R (W) go past Netherwylde Farm, ignore a turning L, at the signpost continue (W). This is a firm wide track with views of the river R. Go past the pumping station R, and follow the wire fence R (W).

5 At the waymark post ignore the turning R, and continue SW on the bridleway towards the overhead power lines. Just before reaching the lines a path goes sharp R (N) over a stile towards the river. Take this clear path, cross the river by the steel bridge, and turn R (NE) along the far bank noting the confluence of the rivers Ver and Colne.

6 Go through the gate into Drop Lane and cross to the gravel footpath and bridleway opposite. Go (N) along this with hedge L to the boundary fence of a Management and Conference Centre. Follow this fence L (NE) past the centre, and the small cemetery L, to the signpost by the car park. Continue R (NE) along the access road, ignore the turning R, go through the strip of woodland (N). Continue along the road to Smug Oak Lane.

7 Cross this lane with care and go through the waymarked gate opposite. Continue (N) with wire fence R. After 100m turn R (E) into a fenced path through into the infill area. In 200m at another waymark turn L (N) ascend the steps and cross the footbridge over the M25. On the far side turn R (E) for a few metres to a waymark post.

8 Turn L at this post and continue (N) with spinney and wire fence R. Eventually this path continues N between wire fences with views over lakes in the old sand quarry. In about 1 km the path makes a short L and R with a good view over the last lake. Go through a gap in the hedge at the waymark, and turn L (W) along Hyde Lane. This goes for about 400m between hedges to a crossing over the railway.

9 Do not cross the railway, but instead turn sharp R (NE) down steps along a clear path just before the railway. This goes along a school boundary (L) and emerges on to the original track in which turn L. Go through the gate into Branch Road, continue (NW) across the playing fields to the start of the walk.

WALK 21

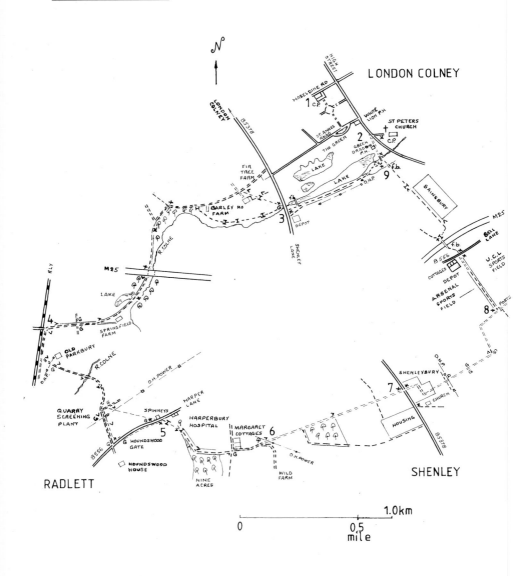

LONDON COLNEY

RADLETT

SHENLEY

1.0km

0 0.5
mile

© Crown copyright

**Total distance 6.5 miles (10.5km)
using the car park at St. Peters
Church 5.7 miles (9.2km)**

LONDON COLNEY, OLD PARKBURY AND SHENLEYBURY

Park in public car park in Haseldine Road, London Colney.
G.R. 177,041 or by St Peters Church. G.R. 182,037

1 Take the asphalt path between housing at rear of car park (SE). Go through the circle of housing to the path opposite (SE) which leads to Sanders Close. Where this meets The Green, turn L along St. Annes Road (NE). At the White Lion PH turn R into the High Street. Bear R before the bridge, go past the Green Dragon PH R. (If using the St. Peters car park, cross the High Street to the Green Dragon PH opposite).

2 Turn L and cross the river by the footbridge. Then turn R at the signpost along a grassy path (W) alongside a hedge and Broad Colney lake R, and a fence and power line L. At the fork in the path ignore the track L, and continue (W) by the lake past the footbridge R, into Shenley Lane.

3 Turn R along the lane, and cross to the signposted gate down steps. This is a permissive path liable to flooding. It is no longer possible to go along the north bank of the river. This path is closed by a wire fence where a large concrete surface water drain from the new housing discharges into the river. Follow waymarked path diagonally (NW) across the field over a stile, keeping Barley Mow Farm L and join bridleway at junction with farm access road. Turn L, continue (W) on firm gravel surface, with views of river L. Where the track turns sharp R, continue ahead (S) along a headland path with fence L overlooking the river. Continue (S) along the river bank under the M25 bridge. On emerging from the bridge, continue (SW) between fences passing a lake R and Springfield Farm L. Continue (W) along the farm access road to the railway bridge.

4 Do not cross the railway, instead turn L along the asphalt road (S) at the side of the railway R. Soon turn L at the waymark under power lines along the access road past Old Parkbury L (SE). Cross the river over a footbridge, and follow a fenced path to an intersection, with quarry workings R. Look out for heavy vehicles, go directly across and continue (S) along the bridleway parallel to the access road R. At the top of the hill cross Harper Lane and turn L. Continue along the asphalt path (NE) to the signpost opposite the house called 'Spinneys'.

5 Turn R, go over a stile and continue along a clear path (SE) towards a strip of woodland. Cross a stile, turn sharp R (SE) into a woodland strip alongside a wire fence L. Ignore a crossing track, continue (E) between wire fences and emerge on to an access road at Margaret Cottages. Continue (E), avoid the fork R leading to Wild Farm, instead take the clear track L up a slope (NE) on to open farm land passing under a power line.

6 Continue (NE) along the track past a wood R into Shenley Lane B5378. An alternative route around the wood and housing is shown on the map opposite.

7 Cross this road into Shenleybury Farm (now office units) along a wide asphalt bridleway (NE) which soon makes a short R and L and continues as a clinker track through a gate. This wide track between hedges turns sharp L by a locked gate, followed by a R turn (NE).

8 At a transverse path marked by metal posts, turn L (NW) along a path with fence L and hedge and ditch R. The path goes between sports fields, L Arsenal and R UCL. Continue into an access road passing a works entrance and cottages L. This meets the B556 Bell Lane. Cross the lane to the track opposite which leads to a footbridge over the M25. At the far side cross the stile R to the boundary fence of Sainsbury R. Turn L (NW) and follow this fence to a stile at the far corner. Cross this, continue (NW) passing a small plantation R. Cross the river at the signposted footbridge.

9 Turn R past the Green Dragon PH to join the start of the walk item 1. Return along the High Street (NW) back to the car park.

WALK 22

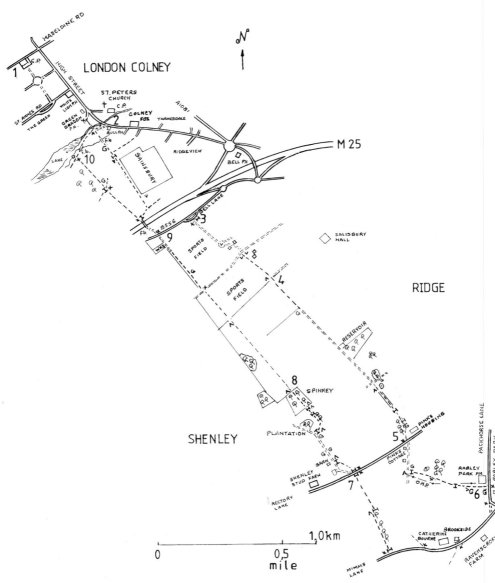

© Crown copyright

**Total distance 6.2 miles (10km) or
the alternative route 5.2 miles (8.4)
Using the car park at St. Peters Chu
5.5 miles (8.8km) or 4.5 miles (7.2)**

LONDON COLNEY, RIDGE AND SHENLEY

WALK 22

Park in public car park in Haseldine Road, London Colney G.R. 177,041
or in car park by St. Peters Church G.R. 182,037

1 Take the asphalt path between the housing at rear of car park (SE). Go through the circle of houses to the path opposite which leads to Sanders Close. Where this meets The Green, turn L along St.Annes Road (NE). At the White Lion PH turn R into the High Street. Continue (SE) then bear R before the bridge to the Green Dragon PH. (If using the car park at St. Peters Church, cross the High Street to the Green Dragon PH.)

2 Turn L (SE) and cross river at footbridge. Cross a brook, and go (SE), with small plantation L. Cross a stile to meet Sainsbury boundary fence L (SE). Continue to waymark L at fence corner. Bear R to a stile and signpost leading to the footbridge over M25. Cross into a gravel track which meets Bell Lane. Turn L (NE) along lane for 100m.

3 At the UCL Sports Ground entrance, turn R through gates and go along the concrete access road to the car park. Bear L across car park past a roundabout with a waymark L. Bear R along a concrete track (SE) passing a house R, with ditch and hedge L. A short R and L on a transverse bridleway leads to a path (SE). Go in front of the sheds L and continue (SE) with hedge L. Go through a hedge gap to another transverse track. Note Salisbury Hall L.

4 Continue ahead uphill along a wide cinder track over fields (SE) towards a wood. This track becomes a concrete access road passing the wood L, then crosses a field (SE) with a small group of trees L to a gap with a waymark. Continue between trees into a grassy path with hedge L, this becomes a wide grass track between hedges, after crossing two stiles a gate leads to a path with fence L and hedge R which emerges on to Rectory Lane at a signpost by Pinks Farm Housing.

5 Turn L along the lane, and in a few metres R along an asphalt access road (S) passing Pinks Cottage R. Just before the road turns L, and at an overhead power line turn L, cross a stile by a gate, and continue (E) under the power line. Pass a small pond L, and in the corner of a wood L go through a gate by a gate. Continue (E) with hedge L, cross a stile, then through a gate with Rabley Park Farm L, go through a kissing gate into Packhorse Lane.

6 Turn R along the lane (S) past Rabley Park L, and Rabley Willow R. Where the road bears L, keep straight on along a short path into Mimms Lane, into which turn R. Continue (SW) past Ravenscroft Farm L, and Catherine Bourne Farm R. In a further 250m is a stile and signpost R (FP18). Cross this into a meadow with a row of trees R (NW). Continue with fence R over a stile to another by a gate into Rectory Lane.

7 Cross the stile and the lane, to the stile opposite into a meadow. Follow the wooden fence L by the farm access road, and when this bears R locate a stile by the large barn. Cross this into a wide access road with a wooden fence on each side. Go downhill (NW) passing gates on each side to a stile with gate R near a small plantation. Cross this and go diagonally to a fence and row of trees R. Continue to a stile in a transverse fence and hedge, cross into a small field, cross another stile ahead into a small spinney. At the far boundary, emerge into farmland.

8 Looking (NW) towards the Sainsbury complex, note a gap in the hedge in the distance. Go straight across the field, passing a hollow L and go through this gap (NW). Cross a small field and continue (NW) through a gap, then along a fenced path into an access road with works entrance and cottages L. Cross Bell Lane.

9 Go along the gravel track and cross the same footbridge as in item 2. On the other side do not cross the stile R, instead continue (NW) along a track with hedge L. Ignore a path L and kissing gate R, and after passing a small copse L, meet a transverse path by a lake.

10 Here turn R (NE) on to the transverse path then with lake L, after 5m turn L at waymarked post to cross a small footbridge and continue to the original path at the Colne footbridge signpost. Cross the steel bridge, turn R to the Green Dragon PH. Turn L, go up the High Street and so back to the car park. **Alternatively** to shorten the walk, at item 5, Pinks Farm Housing, turn R along Rectory Lane (SW) to item 7 at Shenley Stud Farm.

WALK 23

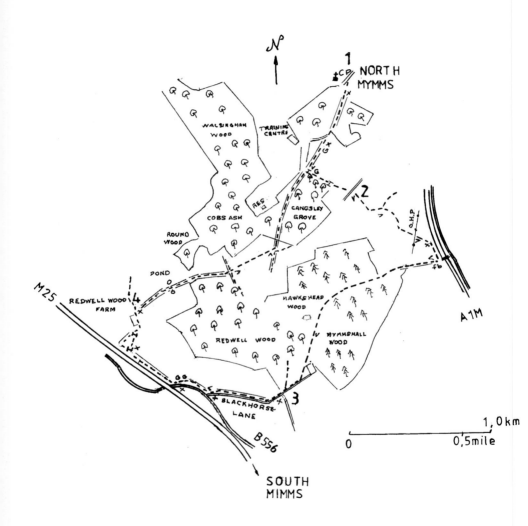

© Crown copyright

Total distance 5 miles (8km)

NORTH MYMMS AND REDWELL WOOD

Park in car park of St Mary's Church, North Mymms

G.R. 222,045   Good views of St Albans from the ridge

1 From the church car park turn R on to the hard surfaced lane (SW). Where the tarmac lane turns R to North Mymms Training Centre, continue through gate along a fenced track to Cangsley Grove. At the gate turn L, cross the stile and follow bridleway (SE) with wood R, to a second stile. Continue to a crossing of paths at hedge ahead.

2 Continue straight ahead (SE) on wide path between hedges, ignore waymarked track L, take the gravel track uphill, keeping hedge L under overhead power line then follow motorway wooden fence to a footbridge over the A1(M). Do not cross, but turn R (W) along path with hedge L, which gently ascends into woodland. At the top of the rise keep to the wider track which veers gradually L (SW) through the woodland, ignoring all minor paths. Soon, after passing an isolated house R, the track descends through the wood towards South Mimms joining a tarmac road Blackhorse Lane.

3 Turn R (W) continue along lane, just before the lane meets the B556 L, bear R (NW) on to a tarmac bridleway. Bear R at the end of bridleway, through an automatic gate on to a concrete road (NW) parallel with the M25. This is a private road but is a public bridleway. Follow this road uphill ignoring stiles R, as it passes through Radwell Wood Farm.

4 Turn R (NE) at signpost when through the farm and continue along wide fenced track, past two ponds then along with wood and ditch R, to a gap in a crossing hedge. Continue downhill (NE) across field to a transverse gravel track. Turn L follow track uphill, then through fenced woodlands downhill to join tarmac road back to North Mymms church.

55

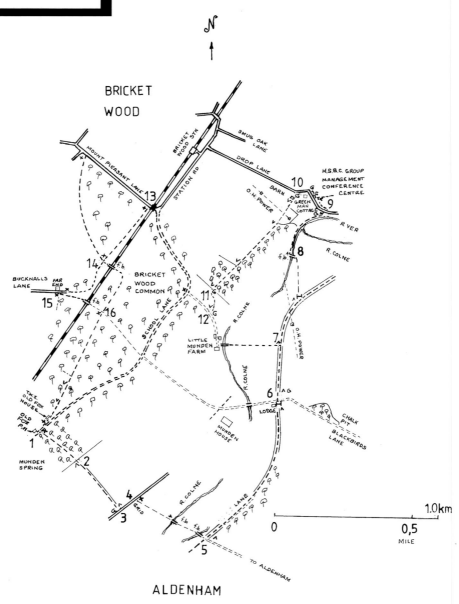

BRICKET
WOOD

ALDENHAM

© Crown copyright

Total distance 5 miles (8km) or by shorter route 4 miles (6.4km)

COLNE VALLEY AND BRICKET WOOD

Park in School Lane, Bricket Wood near The Old Fox public house G.R. 126,003

1 From The Old Fox PH go a few metres (N) and turn R on to a clear path (SE) through the woods.

2 At the boundary fence continue straight on (SE) along a well defined path to a gate.

3 Go through the gate and turn L along the access road leading to Munden House.

4 Immediately after crossing a cattle grid, turn R along a grassy path (SE). This continues across a field to a footbridge over the river Colne, and a second bridge over a flood stream usually dry.

5 In a few metres, at the junction of tracks, turn L (NE) along the lane. Further on note Munden House L.

6 At the Lodge House, turn R along Blackbirds Lane for a diversion to an old chalk pit in a copse L where children can play. Returning to the Lodge, the track continues (N) between hedges. Note Little Munden Farm L.

7 Continue (N) passing under the power lines. After a further 100m, when the bridleway turns (NE), our path turns L (N) to a footbridge over the river Colne.

8 Cross the bridge and turn R along the river bank. After a few metres note the confluence of the rivers Ver and Colne. Continue (NE) into Drop Lane.

9 Cross this lane to a bridleway opposite which goes (N). Where this turns R, a path leads off L at an iron pipe rail. This follows the boundary of the gardens of the HSBC Group Management and Conference Centre. Ignore the first gate L, and go through the second gate L into Drop Lane. Turn R up the lane and at a bend by Green Man Cottage is a gate L. Go through this to an old barn.

10 The path goes to the R of this barn and continues with a fence L (SW). The path leads to a field and crosses it to the corner of the woodland opposite. Continue (SW) along the edge of the wood L, then through a small plantation to a gate in the boundary fence.

11 Go through this gate and the meadow (S) to another gate on to the access road to Little Munden Farm.

12 Turn R (NW) along this road which is a public right of way. At the junction with School Lane turn R (NW). This is a pleasant wooded lane with little traffic.

13 This leads to Mount Pleasant Lane in which turn L, go under the railway bridge, and immediately turn L along a path (SW) which follows the railway boundary fence L.

14 Ignore a crossing path, continue ahead with chain link fence R. The path curves (W) and continues into an asphalt road, Bucknalls Lane.

15 Opposite a house named Far End, another path joins acutely sharp L (SE). Re-enter the woods along this path, keep to the boundary fence L, and cross the railway footbridge. Continue for about 100m.

16 At a shingle filled clearing and a crossing of paths, turn R (SW) and continue through the woods, passing a thatched cottage R called The Old Fox House. Go through the gap in the railing and on to The Old Fox PH, the start of the walk.

Alternatively if starting from Bricket Wood Station, go down Station Road (SW) and start the walk at item 13, returning to the station after item 12.

A shorter walk can be devised by turning L (W) at item 7 along a wide farm track. Cross the concrete bridge at Little Munden Farm, turn R (N) along the access road and rejoin the above route at item 12.

PLACES OF INTEREST

WHEATHAMPSTEAD, BATFORD AND MACKERYE END

WALK 1

1. **THE BULL PH.** A range of timber framed buildings, early C16, with early C17 additions. Tall C17 central stack, opposite to the Mill, incorporating a C16/17 building. Across the river is Wheathampstead Place, a fragment of a large half-H shaped late medieval hall-house. The chief river of Hertfordshire is the Lea, which rises in Luton, Beds, flows across country to Ware, then runs south to the Thames.

3. **LEASEY BRIDGE FARM** - See Walk 6, item 5.

4. **MARQUIS OF GRANBY PH.** C17 timber framed, roughcast, ridge stack, C17/18 single storey wings. The Marquis of Granby (1721-1770) commanded troops in the Seven Years War. After his military career, he established wounded or disabled senior non-commissioned officers as innkeepers.

5. **MACKERYE END** Symmetrical brick front dated 1665, with 'Dutch' gables with pedimented tops and fine stacks. Charles Lamb (1775-1834), essayist and critic, lived here as a child with his great-aunt, Ann Gladman, who was housekeeper. In an older building on the site, John of Wheathampstead, abbot of St Albans (1420-1440), was born.

7. **TURNERS HALL FARM** C16 and C17 house, refaced C19 in flint and redbrick. Cross wing c1500 has a king strut roof.

   THE SLYPE 'Hogs Island' Blackmore End C16 house, moved from St Ippollitts 1928.

8. **TIN POT** C15 or early C16 origins, exposed C16 timber frame at rear wing. Main front is C18 red brick casing.

   GUSTARD WOOD COMMON. Nos 3, 6, 8, 9, 10, & 17 are all C17 or C18 timber framed.

   HERONS FARM early C16 timber framed with C18 red brick casing, and king strut roof. Originally a close studded range of four bays N wing C16, probably a bakehouse. Barn C17.

   THE DELL C18 house, timber framed, weather-boarded, original central ridge stack.

11. **ST HELEN'S** Wheathampstead parish church, mentioned in Domesday Book as Watamstede, C14 largely unchanged since then. Splendid 'Broach' spire, tower c1290. Garrard memorial c1700, floor brasses c1450, alabaster tomb chest of Sir John Brocket, 1558. Well worth a visit.

WHEATHAMSTEAD GUSTARD WOOD AND LAMER PARK

WALK 2

1. **CORN MILL** over river Lea C16/17 timber framed mill, cased 1890-5, now a warehouse.

3. **GUELDERS** C18 wing on R, 1840 main block in yellow gault brick, weather-boarded upper floor.

4. **LAMER HILL GATE** House C17 timber framed, cased in red brick C18, L-shaped, C20 extension.

   Mention is made in Walk 1 (11) of the Garrard memorial. The last member of the family to own Lamer House was Apsley Cherry-Garrard, one of the youngest members of Captain Scott's expedition to Antarctica. He was one of those who found the bodies at the last camp.

REDBOURN, HOLTSMERE END AND STAGS END

WALK 3

1. See Walk 4, item 1.

   To the SW is Church End and St Mary's church with a nave of c1100, tower of c1140, N aisle of 1497, and chancel C15/16. The village moved to the line of the Roman Watling Street to benefit from trade brought by the main road. There are many C17/18 houses.

2. **THE AUBREYS** (Auld-Burh, meaning 'old fort') is an Iron Age defensive fort extending to about 22 acres surrounded by a double bank and ditch on low-lying ground.

3. To the SW is the NE edge of Hemel Hempstead.

   Many of the scattered farms of Redbourn have the suffix 'End', which may suggest a clearing cut in the forest.

6. After passing New Wood, there is a view of St Albans Abbey to the SE.

REDBOURN AND FLAMSTEAD

WALK 4

1. **CRICKET PAVILION** The cricket club was established in 1823, but cricket was possibly played here in 1666. Close by is the old school, now offices, and Redbourn Museum, next to the Cricketers PH, was built for the manager of Woollam's Silk Mill, which was on the site until 1938.

   The Common is an area in excess of 30 acres of semi-natural grassland with several avenues of trees where races and cockfighting were held. CUMBERLAND HOUSE of 1745, is of red brick with Roman Doric door case.

   HIGH STREET AND FISH STREET. There are many interesting houses.

5. **NICHOLLS FARM** C16 or earlier, recased and extended C17, chequered red brick, interior C16 beams and inglenook, S end is C17 outhouse.

ROTHAMSTED AND HARPENDENBURY

WALK 5

4. **ROTHAMSTED MANOR HOUSE** A large imposing red brick mansion mainly 1630 to 1650, incorporating an earlier medieval dwelling, now a hall of residence. The front on S has mullioned and transomed window casements, a three storied porch with Gothic cupola, and Dutch gables. Extended for Sir John Bennett Lawes 1863. He concerned himself with the value of bones as a fertiliser, which led him to produce fertilisers, the profit from which he spent on experiments for enriching the soil. He laid the foundation for scientific agriculture and the Rothamsted Trust.

   NICKY LINE. This railway, opened in 1877, ran from Harpenden, through Redbourn to Hemel Hempstead. Passenger service withdrawn 1947 due to post-war coal shortage, re-opened 1968 by Claydales for transport of Hemelite blocks. Now a footpath called the 'Nicky Line'.

5. **HARPENDENBURY** Farmhouse C15 or early C16 hall house, extended by three bays on S late C17, cross wing mid C19, rear wall has Wealden framing, large central C17 ridge stack. Note the C15 early C16 Tithe Barn.

9. **THE OLD HOUSE** 27 Leyton Road, late C16 known as Bull Inn, late C17 early C18 extension, timber frame exposed at rear, roughcast with brick nogging. C17 stack, wide inglenooks, well preserved house.

   COACH LANE COTTAGE C15 and later, timber framed house on L plan, C17 inserted red brick stack.

   ROTHAMSTEAD MEMORIAL – See Walk 9, item 1.

   WEST COMMON – See Walk 9, item 1.

   FLOWTON PRIORY – See Walk 9, item 1.

   WHITE HORSE PH. – See Walk 9, item 7.

   In mid-C19 the licensee of the Cross Keys established an annual horse race on Harpenden Common, which continued until the First World War. The Silver Cup PH recalls the racing, and the isolated white house on the road to St Albans was formerly the Jockey PH.

NOMANSLAND, HARPENDEN AND WHEATHAMPSTEAD

WALK 6

NOMANSLAND – See Walk 10, item 1.

1. **WEST END FARM** late C17 with early C19 front range, red brick C19 granary at N end. Two barns C18 or early C19 timber framed.

4. **ALDWICKBURY FARM** granary mid C18 red brick, weather-boarded cupola, upper floor has jettied balcony.

5. **LEA VALLEY WALK** Originally Great Northern Branch Railway, which ran from Hatfield to Welwyn, Wheathampstead, Harpenden, Chiltern Green, Luton and Dunstable.

   LEASEY BRIDGE FARM originally a C16 timber framed house with C17 extension, red brick chimney. Single storey bay R, probably a former hall, open–well staircase 1665.

7. **OLD SCHOOL** built 1869, now offices. Polychrome decorated Gothic style, knapped flint walling in zig-zag bonds of yellow gault brick, wooden belfry with leaded spike, dog-tooth eaves.

   ST HELEN'S - See Walk 1, item 11.

WHEATHAMPSTEAD, COLEMAN GREEN AND WATER END

WALK 7

1. See Walk 1, item 1.

2. **DEVIL'S DYKE** About 1,400 feet long and with a maximum depth of 35 feet, forms part of a massive earthwork to the Belgic settlement, which may have been the capital of Cassivellaunus before his defeat by the Romans.

5. **WATER END** The house, said to have been built c1610, lies to the N of the ford. The W brick front has three gables, three two-storeyed bay windows and fine decorated chimney stacks. Originally a manor house of the Jennings family and possibly where Sarah Jennings was born. Waterend Barn in St Albans was moved from the farm in the 1920's.

REDBOURN AND REDBOURNBURY

WALK 8

REDBOURN – See Walk 4, item 1.

1. **NICKY LINE** – See Walk 5, item 4.
3. **HAMMONDS END HOUSE** c1700 dark red brick of five bays and three storeys.
5. **REDBOURNBURY.** Farmhouse, originally a manor house, C15 hall, extended mid C16/17, fine braced arch roof on stone corbels, C17 gabled stair turret at rear and service wing.

    REDBOURNBURY MILL mid C19 extended on W early C19, chequered and plain red brick, mill block has two storey stack hoist, some mill mechanism intact. Disastrous fire August 1987, mill now rebuilt, operational and open to the public
7. **DOOLITTLE MILL** C17 half-timbered, whitewashed building, C17 stack, C18 sash windows. Adjacent barn C18 early C19, has exposed timber frame.

    CHEQUERS PH late C16 early C17 timber framed, painted brick casing, C18/19 N bay rebuilt, C19/20 rear extension. Once part of Fish Street Farm property of Lord Verulam.

HARPENDEN AND HAMMONDS END

WALK 9

1. **ROTHAMSTED MEMORIAL STONE** commemorates 50 years of continuous experiments in agriculture, the first of their kind, by Sir John Bennett Lawes and Joseph Henry Gilbert, 1843/93.

    WEST COMMON Nos. 15 & 16, cottage terrace, C17/18 timber framed core, late C18 red brick casing, N gable and exposed frame, C18 external stack.

    FLOWTON PRIORY early C16 Priory, timber framed, C20 red brick nogging, leaded casements throughout. Building moved from Ipswich 1925.
4. **HAMMONDS END HOUSE** - See Walk 8, item 3.
6. **HATCHING GREEN** No. 1, thatched cottage, late C17, early C18 timber framed with red brick casing, restored C20.
7. **WHITE HORSE PH.** C17 rear wing, front range probably earlier, timber framed, C18 red brick nogging.

NOMANSLAND, SYMONDSHYDE AND COLEMAN GREEN

WALK 10

1. **NOMANSLAND** so named because it was the disputed territory between land owned by St Albans and Westminster Abbeys. It was later the scene of horse racing, prize fighting and cock fighting.

    FERRERS LANE is named after Katherine Ferrers, a young widow turned highwayman, said to have been fatally wounded here. The Wicked Lady PH also recalls her name.

    NOMANSLAND FARM front range c1705, extended at rear c1800, red brick, front has c1800 sash windows. Barns C18 timber framed.
4. **SYMONDSHYDE FARM** farmhouse C17 timber framed, c19 red brick extensions, C17 cross wing.
7. **JOHN BUNYAN'S CHIMNEY.** A C17 chimney stack is all that remains of a cottage where John Bunyan (1628-1688), author of 'The Pilgrim's Progress', is said to have stayed and preached. The cottage and two next to it were demolished in 1877.
8. **OLD BEECH HYDE HOUSE** late C15 hall house, mid C17 cross wing, cased in red brick, large external mid C17 stack, C16 floor beams, 1980 extension on W, connects with C19 barn range.
9. **BEECH HYDE FARM** C16 hall house, T shaped in plan, half timbered, brick faced, C17 ceilings, moulded beams, well preserved brick fireplaces, fine stacks.

REDBOURN TO HOGG END LANE

1. **OLD SCHOOL** - See Walk 4, item 1.
   NICKY LINE - See Walk 5, item 4.
4. **HOGG END** Farmhouse late C16, timber framed, large C17 wing R, late C17 barn L.
5. **BUTLERS FARM** c1700, altered c1830, red brick house square plan. Workshop on W is C17/18.
   KETTLEWELL FARM early C17 half timbered, weather-boarded. Late C18 timber framed barn.
   OLD JEROMES late medieval, timber framed, probably open hall, c1600 stack and fireplaces inserted, bay added on E, C17/18.
6. **SOUTHEND FARM** C17/18 half timbered, brick cased, C18/19 rear extension.
8. **DANE END FARM** mid C18 or earlier red brick, with internal stacks at each end.
   FLOWERS FARM C17 timber framed, re-cased in red brick c1830, C19 extension on NW.
10. **ST MARY'S** - See Walk 3, item 1.
    CHURCH END - See Walk 3, item 1.
    HOLLYBUSH PH. Altered C17, timber framed plastered front, exposed framing at rear.

BATCHWOOD AND CHILDWICK GREEN

2. **BATCHWOOD HALL** Built by Lord Grimthorpe (1816-1905) as a country seat from which he could view the Abbey. The house was greatly altered in 1912.
4. **CHILDWICKBURY** Late C17 built for Joshua Lomax, remodelled 1854 and enlarged c1900 for Sir John Blundell Maple. Stucco on brick, Doric carriage entrance. Coach house and stable court c1890.
   CHILDWICK GREEN St Mary's church and adjoining school, 1867 by Sir George Gilbert Scott, red brick, single aisle. Nos.12-15, 1890 red patterned brick; behind No.15 is a loggia of the former 'One Bell' PH, later a club house. Forge cottage late C17 timber framed house, later a red brick infill. Wellhead on Green late C19, cast iron winding gear intact.
5. **CHILDWICK LODGE** 1897 lodge to Childwickbury, red brick and cream terracotta, stair turret with conical roof, mullioned casements, wrought iron gates.

SANDRIDGE AND AYRES END

6. **POUND FARM** late C15/16, extended and altered C17/18, timber framed, C18 staircase, C18 inserted stack. Two barns, one C15/16, the other C16/17.
   QUEEN'S HEAD PH. 3 dormer single storey, timber framed building C16/17, re-cased mid C19, weather-boarded.
   ST LEONARD'S, Sandridge parish church - See Walk 14, item 3.
7. **THREE HORSESHOES PH.** built as 2 semi-detached cottages, C18, large inglenooks with original curved staircases at each end.

MARSHALSWICK, SANDRIDGE AND SYMONDSHYDE

3. **ST LEONARD'S** Sandridge parish church. Internally there is much of interest, including the Roman bricks in the chancel arch C12, rood screen late C14 and Norman font.

6. **FAIRFOLDS FARM** farmhouse C17, N front refaced in brick C18/19.

7. **FAIRFOLDS FARM COTTAGES** Nos. 1 & 2 Woodcock Hill, originally C15/16 timber framed farmhouse, cross wings C17, with C17 red brick ridge stack.

   CAP'S COTTAGES originally 3 cottages, mid C17, re-cased and extended both ends in late C18, early C19. C19 roughcast, dentilled brick eaves all round.

8. **NASHES FARM** late C17, re-cased in red brick 1888, timber framed, C17 staircase. Attached barn C15/16, probably the shell of an earlier farmhouse.

OAKLANDS, SMALLFORD AND SLEAPSHYDE

1. **SITE OF HILL END HOSPITAL** built 1899 as Hertfordshire County Asylum. St Bartholomew's hospital based here in World War Two, returned to London 1950s - 60s.

   OAKLANDS COLLEGE The Georgian house of 1782 was converted by William Knight in 1844, when the tower was added. Oaklands Park 335 acres, including mansion, cottages, outbuildings, mill and reservoir, bought by Herts CC in 1920 for training agriculture students. New study bedrooms opened 1953. John Innes estate 240 acres at Bayfordbury incorporated in 1967, making total of 650 acres of arable and grass.

2. **OAK FARM HOUSE** C17 timber framed, C19/20 red brick ground floor, large red brick stack R, C17/18 external stack on L, C19 rear extensions. Blocked inglenook.

5. **THREE HORSESHOES PH.** early C18 timber framed, plastered brick casing, C19 extensions L and rear, C20 extension R.

6. **PLOUGH INN** late C17 timber framed, painted brick ground floor, plastered upper, large external red brick stack, 1960 extension L, thatched roof.

   SMALLFORD TRAIL site of old railway, which ran from St Albans Abbey station to Hatfield, opened 1865, closed to passengers 1951. Smallford station now used by scrap metal dealer. Smallford Trail now a footpath and cycleway linking with Alban Way, see Walk 16, item 2.

7. **COLNEY HEATH** originally about 200 acres and known as Tyttenhanger Heath, being owned by the Manor of Tyttenhanger. Early C12 manor given to St Albans Abbey, whose Abbot used it as a country retreat. It is said Henry VIII and Wolsey stayed there during the plague. Tyttenhanger is the site of a lost medieval village, where 31 died of the plague.

LONDON COLNEY, RIVER COLNE AND COLNEY HEATH

2. **ST PETER'S,** London Colney parish church – See Walk 21, item 1.

4. **WOODRAKE COTTAGE** C17/18 timber framed, early C19 casing, weather-boarded, steep pitched roof.

7. **COAL POST** near Church Lane, 1861, to mark limit of coal duty area round London.

8. **TYTTENHANGER PARK** country house, now offices, built c1655, possibly by Peter Mills (1598-1670), altered early C18 and extended, red brick. On front ridge is a large square wooden clock turret surmounted by octagonal bell chamber with cupola.

9. **BULL PH** - See Walk 22, item 2.

10. **TELFORDS BRIDGE** 1774, thought now not to be by Telford, 7 arches.

  WATERSIDE Colne House c1800, stucco porch with Ionic columns. Riverside cottage mid C19. Waterside House C18 timber framed.

  HIGH STREET London Colney, Nos.27,29,31 & 33, C17 timber framed, brick cased later.

COLNEY HEATH AND WILKINS GREEN

WALK
17

1. **COAL POST** on heath, near Queen's Head PH, note City of London crest. This post marked the limit of coal duty area round London.

  QUEEN'S HEAD PH C17/18 timber framed, with C19/20 additions, C19 canted bay window on ground floor, said to have been used to collect coal tax, c1763 inglenook.

3. **SLEAPSHYDE** hamlet known as Slepes Hide 1598. 'Ye Olde House', Nos. 1, 2 & 3 C17, with C19/20 casing, C17 stack.

  SLEAPSHYDE FARMHOUSE early C16 hall house, timber framed, floored late C17, massive central red brick stack, C17/18 service extension with oven stack.

  PLOUGH PH - See Walk 15, item 6.

4. **SMALLFORD TRAIL** - See Walk 15, item 6.

BEDMOND, GRAND UNION CANAL AND NASH MILLS

WALK
18

2. **OVALTINE DAIRY FARM** 1932 by J A Bowden & Partners, black and white building, built as a copy of the dairy farm owned by Marie Antoinette in Versailles. Now converted to private dwellings named Antoinette Court.

9. **GRAND UNION CANAL** Originally named the Grand Junction Canal, built between 1793 and 1805. Chief Engineer William Jessop.

13. **HYDE FARM** mid C16 timber framed, extended C17, cased and extended C18, altered C19/20, C18 external stacks and staircase.

16. **HYDE LANE FARM** late C15 hall bay, timber framed, red brick cased, floored and heated C17, cross wing rebuilt 1977.

POTTERS CROUCH AND MOTORWAY INTERCHANGE

WALK
19

2. **BONE HILL** early Victorian house, on an earlier farm site, since extended each end. Once the home of John Broadwood, piano manufacturer. Bought by Royal National Rose Society 1959, grounds extended 1964, of international fame.

3. **HOLT FARM** farmhouse, open hall C15, altered C16/17, extended at each end C18, timber framed, inserted floor, main beams c1600 of high quality, C17 barn.

  WINCH HILL WOOD part of a triangular site between M25, M1, and A405.

5. **TENEMENTS FARM** C15 medieval hall house, rectangular plan, c1600 ceilings and stack, main stack C17, oven stack C18. Original massive hall tie beam is visible internally.

6. **MILLHOUSE FARM** C16 timber framed, L-shaped, recased and extended late C18, C16/17 stacks and floor beams.

7. **SEARCHES FARM** C15/16 cruck framed farmhouse, C18 red brick cased, C17 central stack. Front sundial 1728.

WHITEHOUSE FARM C16 timber framed, 1788 brick front. Interior open fireplace, C18 staircase.

10. **DANESWICK** farmhouse C17 with exposed timber frame, central ridge stack. Inglenook formerly with staircase attached to stack.

PARK STREET, RIVERS VER AND COLNE

WALK
20

1. **PARK STREET** After departure of Romans, area was known as the hamlet of Parkye.

   HOLY TRINITY CHURCH, Frogmore 1842 by Sir George Gilbert Scott.

2. **MOOR MILL.** The Mill house is c1700, altered in C19. The mill of brick and weatherboarded was added in C19. It has four stable doors, sack hoist doors and hoisting bay. It is now occupied as a restaurant and pub.

4. **NETHERWYLDE FARM** on site known as Netherwelde, late C13, farmhouse C16/17 timber framed, central stack, S front is brick and flint. Interior has open fireplace with cast iron fireback having Arms of James 1, and Jacobean wall painting. Two farm buildings have plaques early C18.

6. **HSBC GROUP MANAGEMENT & CONFERENCE CENTRE** was a farmhouse with late medieval front, C17 rear, C19 additions, exposed timber frame, red brick infill, open hall, C17 staircase, known earlier as Hansteads, home of Lord & Lady Yule, who bred Arab stallions for racing. Tomb of Lord David Yule is on the estate near car park.

LONDON COLNEY, OLD PARKBURY AND SHENLEYBURY

WALK
21

1. **ST PETER'S,** London Colney parish church, a Norman revival church by George Smith of 1825. Glass of E windows designed by Dowager Marchioness of Waterford made 1865.

   GREEN DRAGON PH built as an inn early C17, timber framed, C18 rear extension, and red brick casing. Interior C17 panelling said to be from Salisbury Hall.

2. **BROAD COLNEY LAKES** are a nature reserve with much wildlife. Administered by the Herts and Middlesex Wildlife Trust.

   TYTTENHANGER - See Walk 16, item 8.

3. **NAPSBURY HOSPITAL.** The site of the former hospital was acquired in 1898 by Middlesex CC as the County Asylum. Opened in 1905, it had a rail siding with a link to London. In World War One it was used as a military hospital. Since the closure of the hospital, the site has been developed for housing.

4. **OLD PARKBURY** C15/16 timber framed farmhouse, early C19 casing. Late C17 lateral stack in yellow brick, roughcast rear elevation.

5. **HARPERBURY HOSPITAL** for the mentally handicapped, building started 1928, main building 1934, giving pleasant aspect of separate villas & workshops. Site was initially Porters Park Estate, and used as an aerodrome in World War One. Known in 1930s as Middlesex Colony, renamed Harperbury 1950, later part of the Horizon NHS Trust.

   Between Harperbury and Shenley Lane was the London Colney landing ground used by operational squadrons of the Royal Flying Corps from early 1916 until May 1917. Later used for training.

6. **ST BOTOLPH'S,** which was the parish church, now a house. Built c1424, altered after a fire in 1753. Nicholas Hawksmoor, 1661-1736, buried there. He was employed by Sir Christopher Wren, assisted Vanbrugh at Castle Howard & Blenheim, & built city churches.

On the ridge is the water tower to the former hospital opened in 1934, but now closed. On the site is Porters Mansion, formerly home of Lord Howe and also Hawksmoor.

Seen over the M25 is All Saints Pastoral Centre, begun in 1899. The chapel was added in 1927 by Sir Ninian Cowper. Behind, is the water tower at Napsbury, and on the horizon St Albans Abbey and to its right St Peter's Church.

8. Beside the works entrance is a gate leading to Arsenal Football Club training ground.

LONDON COLNEY, RIDGE AND SHENLEY

WALK
22

2. **BULL PH.** mid C16 timber framed with plastered walls, exposed frame at E end, c1900 canted sash window bays, C17/18 external stack. Inglenook in saloon bar was hidden behind four more recent fireplaces.

3. **SALISBURY HALL**, brick house surrounded by a moat, is a fragment of a house built by Sir John Cuttes, Treasurer of Henry VIII, and altered by Sir Jeremiah Snow about 1670. Nell Gwynne lived in a small lodge when she visited the older house with Charles II.

    Early in World War Two, the Mosquito aircraft was designed and built here.

4. Fine view over St Albans to N, views to Potters Bar to S. To SE at Ridge is grave of Field Marshal Earl Alexander of Tunis (1891-1969), whose family home was at Tyttenhanger.

6. **RABLEY PARK FARM.** Small timber framed C17 house was extended in the C18. Behind is a fine weather-boarded barn.

NORTH MYMMS AND REDWELL WOOD

WALK
23

1. **ST MARY'S** in North Mymms Park existed in the early C14. Between 1328/9, N chapel and N aisle were added with S aisle completed soon after. W tower dates from c1440-50.

    NORTH MYMMS HOUSE is a late Elizabethan house built on the H-plan by Sir Ralph Coningsby. The N front is of two storeys with gabled wings and a central porch. The house passed to the Duke of Leeds and was famous for its collection of paintings.

2. Just S of the footbridge over the A1(M) is the Motte and Bailey castle possibly built by Geoffrey de Mandeville in 1141. The site covers over two acres.

COLNE VALLEY AND BRICKET WOOD

WALK
24

1. **OLD FOX PH.** Mainly C19.

5. **MUNDEN HOUSE** 1787/95 in red brick, remodelled 1828 in stock brick with stone dressings. Interior has well preserved Victoria features.

6. **LITTLE MUNDEN FARM** C17 half-timbered farmhouse.

9. **GREEN MAN COTTAGE** C17 timber framed house with painted brick front, weather-boarded E gable, C18/19 stack.

15. **RAILWAY LINE,** electrified 1988, connects Watford Junction, Garston, Bricket Wood, Park Street and St Albans Abbey. First opened 1858. Bricket Wood station opened 1862.

16. **THE OLD FOX HOUSE** timber framed C17 cottage with thatched roof, lath and plaster wall. Typical Hertfordshire cottage of that period.

BIBLIOGRAPHY

LOCAL INFORMATION

1. Chiltern Hill Walks, Don Hinson, Thornhill Press, 1990

2. Chilterns Illustrated Walks, Trevor Yorke, Countryside Books, 2002

3. The Chiltern Way, Nick Moon, Book Castle, 2000

4. Family Walks, Chiltern North, Nick Moon, Book Castle, 1998

5. Family Walks, Chiltern South, Nick Moon, Book Castle, 1997

6. 24 Footpath Walks in Hertfordshire, Bill Frost (Ed),
    St Albans and District Footpaths Society, 2004

7. Hertfordshire Chain Walk, East Herts FP Society, Castlemead, 1994

8. Hertfordshire Rambles, Liz Moynihan, Countryside Books, 2000

9. The Hertfordshire Way, Bert Richardson, Castlemead, 1998

10. Local Walks – S. Beds and N. Chilterns, Vaughan Basham, Book Castle, 1990

11. Pub Strolls in Herts , Alan Charles, Countryside Books, 2002

12. Pub Walks in Herts, Alan Charles, Countryside Books, 2003

13. Village Walks in the Chilterns, Alan Charles, Countryside Books, 2003

14. Village Walks in Herts, Liz Moynihan, Countryside Books, 2002

15. 100 Walks in Bucks and Herts, Geoff Spreckley, Crowood Press, 1998

16. Walks in Dacorum, Dacorum Borough Council, 1992

17. 50 Walks in Hertfordshire, AA Publishing, 2002

NOTES